The Abrahamic Religions: A Very Short Introduction

VERY SHORT INTRODUCTIONS are for anyone wanting a stimulating and accessible way into a new subject. They are written by experts, and have been translated into more than 45 different languages.

The series began in 1995, and now covers a wide variety of topics in every discipline. The VSI library currently contains over 550 volumes—a Very Short Introduction to everything from Psychology and Philosophy of Science to American History and Relativity—and continues to grow in every subject area.

Very Short Introductions available now:

Available soon:

For more information visit our web site

http://www.oup.com/vsi/

Charles L. Cohen

THE ABRAHAMIC RELIGIONS

A Very Short Introduction

OXFORD
UNIVERSITY PRESS

OXFORD
UNIVERSITY PRESS

Oxford University Press is a department of the University of Oxford.
It furthers the University's objective of excellence in research, scholarship,
and education by publishing worldwide. Oxford is a registered trade mark of
Oxford University Press in the UK and certain other countries.

Published in the United States of America by Oxford University Press
198 Madison Avenue, New York, NY 10016, United States of America.

Library of Congress Control Number: 2019950996

ISBN 978-0-19-065434-4

Printed and bound by CPI Group (UK) Ltd, Croydon, CR0 4YY

Contents

List of illustrations

Acknowledgments

A fleeting paragraph cannot adequately express my personal and professional gratitude. Nancy Toff, my editor at Oxford, believed in the project from its inception. The College of Letters & Science at the University of Wisconsin–Madison allowed me a year's research leave; the Michael and Susan Newburger Foundation provided additional financial support. Without Jennifer Ratner-Rosenhagen, scholar and intellectual muse, I would not have conceived this endeavor, much less essayed it. Everyone who touched the Lubar Institute for the Study of the Abrahamic Religions made it one of my life's most vivifying experiences. I necessarily (and happily) rely on scholars who have dedicated themselves to illuminating one or more of these traditions, including the anonymous readers. Space prohibits citing everyone's contributions. My colleagues in and beyond the University of Wisconsin–Madison have given generously of their time and expertise. What I owe my wife, Christine Amber Schindler, goes beyond telling. She still channels God's love in our relationship—even if we disagree on how to date it.

Preface

Abraham is a figure from antiquity; stories about the putative discoverer of the One God contain material that may date from the third millennium BCE. His name entered Old English from Hebrew as early as the eleventh century CE, although the term "Abrahamic" did not appear in its original sense—"relating to, or characteristic of the biblical patriarch, Abraham"—until 1699. "Abrahamic" in this book means principally "belonging to the group of religions comprising Judaism, Christianity, and Islam, which trace their origin to Abraham," a twentieth-century usage. This definition updates the commonplace observation that Judaism, Christianity, and Islam—the "Abrahamic religions"—are somehow closely related. Not everyone likes this expression or its categorical implications. Some scholars object that the term "Abrahamic" can mislead, especially insofar as it may exaggerate the three religions' similarities and the likelihood that Jews, Christians, and Muslims can set their differences aside. Others regard the categorization itself as incoherent, given adherents' fundamental divisions over matters such as what scriptures they consider canonical and how they understand God's nature.

But relegating Judaism, Christianity, and Islam to separate spheres discounts their affinities. Even as they strove to differentiate themselves polemically, they acknowledged that they shared a common deity and took notice of each other's sacred

1

texts. By the seventh century BCE, a passage in the future Jewish Bible already proclaimed: "Hear, O Israel. The LORD [is] our God, the LORD alone" (Deut. 6:4). Few early Christians spurned these writings or rejected the God they unveiled. Rather, Christianity embraced both while advancing a counterclaim: Jews did not worship the wrong god(s) but had gotten God wrong, failing to recognize His incarnation. Islam, in turn, accepted *Tawrat* (the Torah) and *Injil* (the Gospel) as valid revelations, but asserted the Quran's primacy. Muslims accused Jews and Christians of corrupting their own holy books and denying that Muhammad was the ultimate prophet, but nonetheless allowed that their rivals also worshipped the One God. Meanwhile, Jews looking over their shoulders at Christians and Muslims upheld the integrity and superiority of their own formulations, as did Christian apologists (defenders of the faith). These disputes often displayed the rancor characteristic of civil wars—or frays between members of an extended religious family.

One can classify Judaism, Christianity, and Islam variously. From one perspective, they are monotheisms, religions that uphold God's singularity. Islam itself provides another view, linking them by a tradition of continued divine revelation disclosed in scripture and culminating in the Quran. Muslims regard Jews and Christians as "People of the Book"—a name that outside observers occasionally apply to Muslims too. As apt as these designations may be, however, they do not entirely differentiate these three religions from others. Sikhism and ancient Egyptian Atenism, for example, also qualify as monotheisms, and Muslims came to include Zoroastrians and Hindus as other "People of the Book." The most useful term for collating Judaism, Christianity, and Islam into a single category is "Abrahamic," which distinguishes them by stressing the significance they accord Abraham: Israel's founding patriarch for Jews, guarantor of the covenant for Christians, and a prophet for Muslims. Their Abrahamic identities unite the religions conceptually, even while frequently polarizing their adherents.

1. Abraham cradles his descendants in this illumination from the twelfth-century Bible of Souvigny. Since the late twentieth century, this image has been used to emphasize how Jews, Christians, and Muslims spring from a common ancestor and belong to a shared "Abrahamic" tradition.

To observe that Jews, Christians, and Muslims believe they worship the same God does not imply that their traditions preach the same message. Although the ethics of the world's religions may converge, their doctrines, laws, and mythologies do not. Nevertheless, the fact that Judaism, Christianity, and Islam so readily reference one another while speaking about the One God suggests how closely linked they are. They express this connection in the language of divinity, but its foundations are historical. More than doctrine or even an overlapping vision of Abraham, they share an association through time. Hence I approach them as a historian, respecting their faith commitments without judging them.

The Abrahamic religions have taken shape across the centuries substantially in relationship to one another. Many people tend to regard them as self-contained phenomena formed primarily by their own internal intellectual and institutional dynamics. That their adherents have constructed their identities by maximizing their distance from one another only reinforces this perception. Scholarly and popular accounts ordinarily (and understandably) focus on either Judaism, Christianity, or Islam. Nevertheless, this book presumes that braiding together the histories of the Abrahamic religions reveals a fresh perspective. By moving from one tradition to another, featuring both their intersections and parallel developments, it seeks to foster the habit of never thinking about one without calling the others to mind. The narrative tries to both model and instill this reflex by weaving separate strands into a larger design without sublimating any thread.

Interlacing these histories reveals the importance of politics. The fact that Christianity and Islam have been far more associated with state power than has Judaism has had important consequences for how the traditions evolved and how their adherents treated one another. The term "Abrahamic religions" is itself embedded in politics. The phrase gained currency during

4

and after the 1990s, as conflicts around the world subjected the relationships between them to intense scrutiny. One line of analysis has posited that Judaism and Christianity belong to one civilization, that Islam belongs to another, and that antagonism between the two sides is endemic, perhaps inevitable. This characterization may seem natural given global political alignments in the early twenty-first century, yet, when viewed historically, the idea that Judaism and Christianity belong to a single cultural complex looks rather odd.

Indeed, for virtually all of their mutual existence, Christians and Jews considered themselves separate groups and wanted little interaction. The idea of a Judeo-Christian civilization is a twentieth-century creation, one result of which has been a massive reconsideration of Christianity's Jewish origins. The phrase "Abrahamic religions" connotes a category founded on the three traditions' practice of invoking Abraham, but this book further deploys it to consider Islam as being less alien to the Jewish and Christian worldviews than one might suppose. Any conclusion that Islam belongs to a different civilization than do Judaism and Christianity should emerge (if at all) only after long consideration about their intertwined pasts, rather than be asserted as an axiom.

To contemplate, much less write, a history of Judaism, Christianity, and Islam over the course of three millennia is an exercise in modesty, if not fatuity. No one can possibly master all the materials and necessary skills. The literature is so vast, and the interpretive controversies so pervasive, that virtually any statement is subject to contradiction. I know how little I know about these subjects and how much I have omitted or condensed. Humility notwithstanding, I offer this volume so that readers will think of Judaism, Christianity, and Islam as constituting a family of traditions whose intersections have been, and will likely continue to be, complex. Ever since Christians and then Muslims joined Jews in asserting the primacy of Abraham's One God, they have lived within one another's gravitational fields. The varying political contexts in which they have operated have had much to do with their trajectories, both individual and collective. Setting these traditions in dynamic juxtaposition emphasizes their identities as changing historical phenomena, however much each may claim singular possession of eternal truth. There may be one God, but there is no single Judaism, Christianity, or Islam.

Chapter 1
The Jewish matrix
(1200 BCE–70 CE)

Ancient Israel's discovery of the One God and the religion that developed around that awareness were deeply influenced by the course of its political and cultural relationships with its neighbors. The texts that would constitute the Jewish sacred scriptures embed theological interpretations of this history. As the religion evolved, it was further affected by Jews' dispersion from their heartland, their engagement with Hellenism, and their implication in the eastern Mediterranean's imperial conflicts. By the time of Jesus, Judaism had assumed multiple forms—as would Christianity and Islam.

Biblical Israel (ca. 1200 BCE–ca. 400 BCE)

In the beginning, Tanakh (the Hebrew Bible) tells us, the Jewish people sprang from a migrant family who settled in Canaan—which became *Eretz Yisrael*, the holy land that the One God promised them forever. Their descendants moved into Egypt, where they joined the pharaohs' labor force but remained an unassimilated minority. After revolting against their enslavement, they solidified an identity as *Am Yisrael* (the "People of Israel"), a community forever committed to the God who had liberated them. Having reoccupied their ancestral homeland, they formed successively a loose confederation of tribes, a monarchy, and—under kings David and Solomon—an empire whose capital,

Jerusalem, boasted an ornate temple, the focal point of cultic worship.

Centralization, however, bred discontent about taxes, political favoritism, and the temple priesthood's power. The consolidated monarchy split into the northern and southern kingdoms of Israel and Judah, tiny polities felled by stronger neighbors: Israel by Assyria (721 BCE) and Judah by Babylonia (587 BCE). Members of the northern kingdom were forcibly relocated and lost their identity as Israelites, but the deported Judahites elaborated their religious traditions in exile. When the Persians overran Babylonia (539 BCE), Emperor Cyrus released those who wished to settle in Yehud (Persian Judah), where they reconstructed Jerusalem, built a new temple, and defined themselves as the true People of Israel.

This epic still commands substantial support, but recent advances in literary theory, archaeological exploration, and social scientific method have led many scholars to radically challenge Tanakh's credibility as a guide to the past. Its stories, they charge, are theological and propagandistic, not factual; excavated data, they say, are more reliable. Such criticism has destabilized the classic account. Some newer perspectives contend that Israelite society arose from the gradual consolidation of communities indigenous to hill-country Palestine, not from external invasion. The sagas of David and Solomon wildly exaggerate their conquests and magnificence. The postexile reconstitution of the Temple and religious life involved far more interaction with those who had remained behind than Tanakh lets on. Some revisions surely go too far; the memory of fleeing Pharaoh's chariots, for example, became too intrinsic to Israelite identity for scribes to have fabricated it entirely. Tanakh does contain historical material, especially as one moves forward from the tenth century BCE, but it does not depict a baseline narrative that needs only minor adjustments to its generally accurate trajectory.

At the same time, Tanakh's theological interests do make it the most informative source for tracing Israel's evolving conceptions of God. The Lord to whom they devoted themselves fused at least two figures: El, the high god of the Canaanite pantheon, and YHWH, a warrior god originally associated with people who had entered Canaan from the south. The People of Israel understood their relationship with God as a covenant, an agreement stipulating mutual obligations. While this form was a political commonplace in the ancient Near East, its use to articulate the relationship between a people and their deity seems to have been unique to them. The two most important covenants in Tanakh involve God's pacts with Abraham and Moses. The former assigns Abraham's offspring a permanent homeland; the latter stipulates that the People of Israel belong to the Lord who led them from bondage and commanded their obedience. God will bless them if they comply and punish them if they refuse.

Recognizing a supreme divinity did not, however, translate immediately into conceiving one universal God. Israelites first took YHWH/El as their own while sometimes continuing to worship other people's deities as well. God could be described as heading an assembly of divine beings, but the Lord also sentences its members to death for "showing favor to the wicked" (Ps. 82:2). The prophets frequently express these twin themes: God is both virtuous and unique. This characterization of a single God who upholds moral standards ("ethical monotheism") surfaced strongly in light of the theological and military problems that Assyria posed. Did that empire's devastating triumph discredit God for having betrayed or failed Israel? "No," answered the prophets. God rules the nations, disposes their affairs justly, and deploys foreign powers as agents to rebuke Israel's iniquities. By the sixth century, this conclusion had become axiomatic. Consoling the exiles, the anonymous "Second Isaiah" reverenced "The Creator... who alone is God" and who will reduce Babylon for having shown Israel "no mercy" (Is. 45:18, 47:5, 6).

The actual exercise of Israel's relationship with God began with the king and was managed by a hereditary priesthood. During the monarchical period, public devotions took place at various shrines, and the Jerusalem Temple eventually became the supreme focus of state-sanctioned ceremony. The principal rite—public and private—was animal sacrifice. Tanakh glosses over the underlying rationales, but, at its root, such sacrifice was intended to repair a divine–human relationship disordered by the supplicants' impure acts. During the three annual pilgrimage festivals—Passover (in the spring), Shavuot (summer), and Sukkot (fall)—Israelites brought harvest offerings to the Temple. Individuals might also contact God through the medium of a prophet, frequently a cultic official, who was thought to convey divine messages about matters that ran from finding lost items to fashioning royal policy. Reverence for God mixed with devotion to other deities. The use of figurines associated with Asherah/Astarte, an ancient Middle Eastern goddess who in the Israelite context sometimes appears as YHWH's consort, bespeaks widespread resort to a feminine power on matters of fertility. The Omride dynasty's Baal worship, so savaged by the writers of 1 and 2 Kings, can be understood as a syncretism undertaken partly for diplomatic and political reasons rather than a rejection of YHWH outright.

Exile and restoration had impacts on belief, observance, and religious identity that can be discerned even if the forces shaping them remain obscure. Competitors to the One God dropped away; adoration of figurines vanished. Israel's sense of its covenantal obligations came to include not simply ritual performance but, more importantly, each individual's internalized commitment to ethical behavior, a change signified by Jeremiah's proclamation of the "new covenant" in which God "will put My Teaching into their inmost being" (Jer. 31:33). By ca. 400 BCE, roughly when Tanakh's historical material ends, a religious community, the self-acknowledged heir of Biblical Israel, had unified itself around a collective self-understanding that distinguished it from its neighbors. That identity included lore about how the God of nations had covenanted with them and guided their history, an attachment to the land God had deeded them, distinctive customs (such as infant male circumcision and a prohibition against eating pork), a common language, and shared worship. Religious life revolved around the Temple, not sacred scripture, and presumed that its rituals were secured by either an Israelite government or a foreign ruler disposed to protect it. We can begin to call these people "Jews" (*Yehudim*), a name derived from "Yehud" and used in some of Tanakh's late-written books. It is, however, too early to speak of a coherent "Judaism," at least if that designation denotes the liturgical centrality of the Torah, much less of Tanakh, the whole of which did not yet exist. Future Judaisms would build on the historical and religious materials melded in Yehud, even if future Jews—not to mention Christians and Muslims—would configure those materials in rather disparate ways.

Tanakh

The Hebrew Bible is called "Tanakh," a title that amalgamates its collective parts: *Torah*, *Nevi'im* (Prophets), and *Ketuvim* (Writings). Tanakh preserves and interprets the historical, cultural, and religious heritage of Israel and Judah. In its current form, it serves as both the definitive anthology that constitutes Judaism's holy scriptures and a pillar of Jewish religious life, but these roles postdate its compilation. Tanakh accrued literary authority only when Jewish intellectuals in Hellenistic Egypt began to credit texts with greater significance than priestly pronouncements or prophetic utterances, and it achieved its current form only after the destruction of the Second Temple in 70 CE. Parsing its composition history can be quite puzzling. Depending on which estimate one follows, as many as eight centuries may have elapsed between the transcribing of Abraham's story and Daniel's. Many of the books consist of snippets patched together—a genealogy with, say, a legal list. Most of them were created or edited by scribes, court officials who performed diplomatic, administrative, clerical, and academic tasks. Few were meant to be literary, and none was intended to be holy. The attributed authors are almost all fictive, with figures like Moses or David cited to boost the writings' stature.

Although the Old Testament contains the same books as Tanakh does, their internal arrangement differs. The former organizes them roughly by genre, the latter in a tripartite scheme based generally on their chronological appearance. Both compilations begin with the Torah—which normally refers to the "Five Books of Moses" (or Pentateuch), though the name can extend to the entire Tanakh and even beyond. "Torah" can be construed as "law," but to prioritize this sense assumes the perspective of early Christians, who regarded Jewish devotion as fixated on obeying divine law and thus insufficient for salvation. For Jews, the broader meaning of "Torah" is "teaching" or "instruction." Its organizing narrative relates the People of Israel's fortunes from the time of their progenitor, Abraham, until they stand along the River Jordan poised to conquer Canaan; it also contains myths, cosmology, genealogies, and poetry, as well as legal codes.

Its textual inconsistencies, manifest in antiquity, were frequently explained in the twentieth century by the "documentary hypothesis," according to which the Torah consists of four main sources: one set of traditions from the Kingdom of Judah; another from the Kingdom of Israel; a theologized chronicle associated with the religious reforms of King Josiah in seventh-century Judah (the "Deuteronomistic history"); and a body of ritual and legal injunctions prescribed during (or after) the exile. This consensus has collapsed under claims that the composition process was more multilayered, gradual, and accretive than the documentary hypothesis suggests or that trying to find coherence in the underlying source material is impossible. Although no longer gospel, the assumption that multiple sources underlie the Torah can still help clarify many of the text's contradictions. Some version of it existed in 458 BCE, when Ezra, a Jewish priest in the

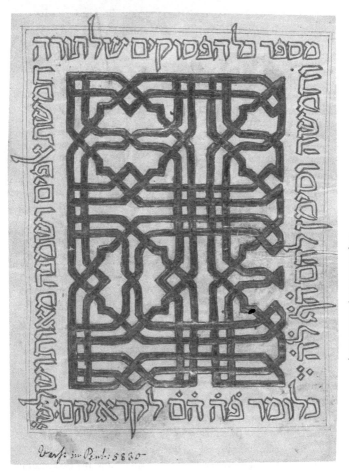

2. A decorative carpet page marks the end of Deuteronomy in a fourteenth-century Hebrew Pentateuch. Such illumination—common where Jews had extensive interactions with Muslims—reflects the nonfigurative motifs widespread in Islamic architecture and art.

Persian emperor's service, read it to the Yehudites in Jerusalem, but that scroll included less than what exists today.

Tradition divides *Nevi'im* into two parts. The "Former Prophets" relate Biblical Israel's history from the invasion of Canaan to the Babylonian Exile, emphasizing how apostasy portends disaster while repentance brings deliverance. The fifteen books of the "Latter Prophets," with one exception, convey divine pronouncements: oracles, counsel, and predictions of calamity should Israel fail to heed God's word. These prophets criticized unjust and unethical behavior, sparing neither rulers nor subjects. Prophecy had a long history in Biblical Israel, but Tanakh preserves expressions only from the era between the Kingdom of Israel's impending demise and the godly community's restoration in Jerusalem (ca. 750–ca. 420 BCE), during which time prophets outside the cult became particularly public figures. Each oracle deals with a specific historical moment, but all proclaim God's blameless government of the world and the necessity for human beings to behave justly.

Ketuvim is an eclectic assemblage whose parts are usually taken to have been composed between the sixth and second centuries BCE, although some psalms are doubtless older. The corpus lacks either a unifying narrative framework like the Torah's drama of national creation or a consistent moral urgency like the prophets' calls to repent. Some prominent concerns do appear if one loosely classifies the works by genre. Job, Proverbs, and Ecclesiastes exemplify wisdom literature, "advice books" dealing with matters of universal human import. Ezra, Nehemiah, and the two volumes of Chronicles are theological histories, while Ruth, Esther, and Daniel might be considered historical novellas meant to instill moral, didactic, and spiritual lessons. *Ketuvim* also includes a range of poetry: doleful in the case of Lamentations, which mourns Jerusalem's ruin, erotic in the case of Song of Songs— perhaps an old marriage liturgy. Psalms runs the gamut of spiritual affections from deepest contrition to profound confidence in the Lord, "my shepherd" (Ps. 23:1). Hard to contextualize and harder to date, these chants originally served the Temple cult, but Jews and Christians have long incorporated them into personal devotions. Muslims—while likewise reverencing them as revelation (Quran 4:163)—ordinarily have not.

Tanakh's mélange nonetheless displays a consistent view of how divinity works. It insists that the Lord cares deeply about human beings and watches over them ceaselessly. Unlike modern historians, who analyze the proximate reasons why things happen and strive for even-handedness, biblical writers reflected on events' ultimate meanings and sided with those who promoted the One God's worship against backsliders and idolaters. This perspective yielded the radical insight that God evaluates human behavior morally and favors the just, even though they may not triumph in this world like the Assyrians and Babylonians—victors who, according to adage, write history on their own terms. Tanakh, contrarily, tracks a people whose God lets their enemies despoil their holiest sanctuary to punish their sins. Yet the covenant endures, both on God's side and, more strikingly, on Israel's, which trusts the Lord even in the agony of defeat. Tanakh also reveals Israel itself: a national family descended from a line of patriarchs, rooted in *Eretz Yisrael*, and affirmed by lived experience divinely inflected at every step.

Christians would accept this corpus into their own scripture, though they would read it for presentiments of Christ, and Muslims would recognize Muhammad as descending from its prophetic stock. Both, of course, would interpret Israel and its relationship with God differently than would Jews.

Diaspora and Hellenism (ca. 600 BCE–ca. 50 BCE)

As in Biblical Israel, cultural exchanges and regional power configurations continued to influence Jews and their religion in the centuries following the Temple's reconstruction, but they operated on a people no longer massed in a circumscribed space. East of *Eretz Yisrael*, a portion of the Babylonian exiles elected to remain in Persian Mesopotamia, founding communities that would grow into one locus of Jewish life. Egypt formed another hub. Collectively, Jewish settlements outside the Holy Land are called the "diaspora" (Greek, "dispersion"), a term that usually (as here) includes all Jews, whether they migrated freely or not. By the first century CE, Jews living abroad had long outnumbered those inhabiting the Holy Land. The diaspora's existence inaugurated an ongoing, pregnant dynamic for Judaism and Jewish identity. On the one hand, *Eretz Yisrael*, especially Jerusalem, maintained its emotional resonance and ritual importance; diaspora Jews flocked to the Temple for the pilgrimage festivals and, in the later second century BCE, began to pay annual half-shekel contributions toward its support. For some, particularly after the Second Temple's destruction, the homeland beckoned as the place of return, a distant object of longing. At the same time, diaspora Jews seem to have experienced little dissonance between the respect they accorded the Holy Land and the loyalty they paid their own communities and governments.

Judaism had developed primarily among the Semitic-speaking peoples of the ancient Near East, but it encountered a very different ethos after Alexander the Great had, by 329 BCE, conquered the Jewish homeland (now called Judea) and the diaspora territories. Incorporation into Alexander's empire exposed Jews to Hellenism, a cultural complex based on the language, thought, customs, religion, and art of ancient Greece. According to one line of argument, Hellenism represented an alien system whose every inroad corrupted Jewish institutions and beliefs, but this interpretation posits Judaism as a self-contained monolith. One might better understand its interaction with Hellenism as an example of how Jews (not to mention Christians and Muslims) absorb influences from their surroundings to enrich their own traditions while maintaining (to their satisfaction) foundational convictions and customs. Although a handful of Hellenized Jews may have renounced their faith and a few traditionalists may have rejected Hellenic culture completely, most Jews accommodated it to some degree. In Jerusalem, the second-century scribe Simeon ben Sira wrote a book of ethical maxims exhibiting Greek idioms and ideas while affirming that all wisdom is "the law that Moses commanded us" (Ecclus. 24:23). In Alexandria, the center of Hellenistic Jewish learning, the first-century philosopher Philo read scripture allegorically, a method inflected by Stoicism. Hellenistic culture affected every facet of Jewish life, and Jews appropriated it into their self-reflections, but its habits of mind did not infiltrate the enduring structures of Jewish religious thought as they did those of Christianity.

One of Hellenistic Jewry's signature achievements was the Septuagint, the translation of Tanakh into *Koine* (common) Greek. Compiled between the third and first centuries BCE, it almost certainly represents the work of Alexandrian Jewry, who needed scripture in Greek because they no longer spoke or wrote Hebrew. The Septuagint makes some formal changes, reordering books and including new material. Its existence offers witness to the religious power that Jews in the last centuries BCE were according written texts, a significant moment in the process by which Jewish identity embraced the Torah and Judaism became a "religion of the book." Even so, the Septuagint has arguably had greater abiding significance for Christianity than for Judaism. The Old Testament used it, rather than Tanakh, for a basis; New Testament writers quoted it (rather than Hebrew versions). Catholics and Orthodox Christians would accept its additions as a second set of fully authoritative (deuterocanonical) books. Most Protestants would not, although some printed them in a separate section of their Bibles. The early Church forged its principal doctrines in conversation with it. The legend that seventy-two translators "harmoniously" produced identical copies has a Christian provenance: Epiphanius, a fourth-century bishop who defended the Septuagint's superiority against later Jewish revisions. As its importance for Christians rose, Jews abandoned it to assert the sole legitimacy of the Hebrew text.

The religion of Biblical Israel developed first in conditions of self-determination, then of exile, and finally of mild toleration and limited self-autonomy under the Persians, circumstances that continued under Alexander and his successors until the reign of Antiochus IV (r. 175–164 BCE), who feared that Judea had rebelled against him. In reprisal, he erected a statue of Zeus in the Temple and forbade Jews from observing the Torah. This unprecedented intervention—the first instance in antiquity of an adversary targeting a religion rather than a polity—triggered a revolt led by Mattathias and Judah Maccabee. Beginning as a religious resistance movement, it had within a decade transformed into a national liberation campaign that established a kingdom ruled by the Hasmonean dynasty (140–37 BCE). The revolt has frequently been seen as a rejection of Hellenization, but the Maccabees counted Hellenized Jews as supporters and adopted Greek political customs.

Created as a byproduct of the effort to restore traditional religious practices, the only independent Jewish state in *Eretz Yisrael* between 587 BCE and 1948 CE paradoxically contributed to their erosion. In the short run, Hasmonean policies, including unification of the monarchy with the high priesthood in a single person, generated partisan dissatisfactions with the Temple cult. In the longer run, factional struggles within the state brought a new power into Judean politics—with catastrophic consequences. Simeon Maccabee sought Roman support against the Greek Seleucids; by 6 CE, Rome itself ruled the territory—now the province of Judaea. The Romans preferred to grant their subjects religious autonomy, and Jews under imperial rulers had ordinarily been quiescent, but tensions in Judaea escalated in the first century CE, culminating in the Temple's ruin.

Second Temple Judaism(s) (538 BCE–70 CE)

Even as sacred texts rose in Jews' esteem, the Second Temple remained central to their religious identity. A modest structure when first completed with Persian support, the edifice and its compound gradually expanded under Jewish and Gentile (non-Jewish) rulers alike. By the Hasmonean period, the Temple's systems for managing water allowed 700 *kohanim* (priests) to conduct sacrifices on an industrial scale; the staff included levites (functionaries who chanted psalms, guarded gates, and maintained the physical plant), scribes, and other officials. Herod the Great (r. 37–4 BCE) inaugurated the grandest reconstruction, which doubled the holy precinct's size. Huge restraining walls girded a platform on which rose nested courts of progressively greater sanctity, culminating in the Holy of Holies, God's earthly dwelling. Within one of the Roman Empire's largest public spaces, people crowded the outermost Court of the Gentiles to consult priests, exchange money to purchase sacrificial animals, deposit offerings, hear preachers, and socialize. At sunrise, according to the contemporary Jewish historian Flavius Josephus, the Temple's gilding shone so brightly that onlookers had to avert their eyes. The product of state sponsorship as well as private donations from both *Eretz Yisrael* and the diaspora, such magnificence magnified the Temple's symbolic importance and the priestly aristocracy's status.

Notwithstanding the preeminence of cultic observances, religious life during the Second Temple era increasingly emphasized personal duties to purify oneself, follow the Torah, and perform daily rites. Jews prayed in both public and private, beyond as well as within Jerusalem. Scripture study emerged as a principal function of a new local institution, the synagogue. Injunctions for holy living (like dietary prohibitions) multiplied. This shifting emphasis toward God's relationship with Jews individually, as opposed to Israel collectively, was manifested theologically by an intensified interest in the workings of God's justice and personal redemption, stimulating heated speculation about resurrection, free will, and eternal judgment. In some circles, apocalyptic (Greek, "revelation") theories explaining evil's persistence and Jews' subordination posited a final war between the righteous and the wicked in which the former would triumph, led by a messiah (*mashiach*, "anointed one") who was ordinarily conceived as a transcendently powerful human figure and occasionally as a cosmic one. Still, Jews coalesced around their rules of conduct, not their beliefs.

Most Jews adhered to the Second Temple cult and its prescriptions to varying degree, but murmurs that the priests were corrupt and the Temple was polluted grew louder during and after the Hasmonean dynasty. Josephus identified three main oppositional sects: Pharisees, Sadducees, and Essenes. Alike in disparaging the Temple hierarchy, invoking the Torah, and attracting men from the upper social orders, these disputants disagreed primarily about law and hermeneutics (methods of biblical interpretation) while also arguing about philosophical and political matters. Pharisees were laypeople (and priests) who accepted ancestral traditions along with the Torah as legitimate guides for determining proper conduct, gained a reputation for fastidious legal observance, and believed, among other things, in bodily resurrection. Sadducees were priests and aristocrats who subscribed only to textual authority to guide proper observance and denied bodily resurrection.

Essenes formed communities that followed ascetic regimens in pursuit of purity, denounced fellow Jews for religious laxity, condemned the *kohanim* for following an errant ceremonial calendar, and lived in apocalyptic expectation of a final conflict in which the forces of light (they themselves) would overcome the armies of darkness. Josephus also mentioned a "fourth sect," less a coherent category than a catch-all rubric that included *Sicarii* and the Zealots—both of whom mixed revolutionary politics with radical religious ideology—as well as common bandits. Materializing in the 40s CE, the *Sicarii* assassinated Jews suspected of collaborating with the Romans; their mass death defending Masada in 73 CE ended the Great Revolt against Rome. The Zealots seem to have cohered in 67 CE from among the peasantry fleeing Vespasian's army; they led the resistance to the siege of Jerusalem, where most of them died.

The Roman Empire allowed subject populations religious autonomy on condition of political docility, but because Romans expected greater conformity to their own cultural and political norms than had the Persians and Greeks, Jews found assimilation particularly difficult, especially given the imperium's distaste for Jewish religious customs. Aggravated by Roman administrative incompetence and Jewish restiveness over Gentile paganism, this antagonism underwrote deteriorating relations. In Egypt, one governor allowed Alexandrians angry about Jewish demands for citizenship rights to defile synagogues and kill Jews with impunity. In Judaea, social and economic pressures intensified against a background of endemic violence and currents of religious nationalism excited by memories of independence and hopes that a messiah would redeem Israel from foreign oppressors. The stresses gave way in 66 CE, when the governor crucified Jews who protested his withdrawals from the Temple treasury; in retaliation, priests eliminated sacrifices for the emperor's welfare, precipitating raids by Jewish rebels, followed by a massive Roman counterattack. The war's climax came in Jerusalem, now stuffed with refugees, where radical factions dedicated to vanquishing the Romans (while liquidating their internal rivals) incinerated food supplies, forcing a fight to the death. After a months-long siege, Roman legions scaled the walls, killed or captured virtually everyone inside, and razed the Temple so thoroughly that "every part" of its hill, Josephus reported, appeared in flames.

Defeat, exile, and restoration had altered ancient Israel's religion, but the Second Temple's obliteration, coupled with Jews' declining status in the Roman Empire, would force a far greater reconstruction. Lacking a single agreed-upon holy place, modern Christians, however empathetic, may have difficulty imagining the magnitude of the liturgical renovations that the Temple's loss demanded, though Orthodox Byzantines watching Hagia Sophia—their monumental cathedral—reconfigured as a mosque certainly could. Muslims contemplating a hypothetical demolition of Mecca's Masjid al-Haram (Sacred Mosque) and the consequent disruption of the *hajj* (pilgrimage) may be able to entertain a more visceral understanding of what the Second Temple's loss portended for Judaism.

Yet to designate the Second Temple's cult the sole "authentic" Judaism overlooks both communities that practiced alternative observances and the intellectual ferment that animated the literatures of wisdom and apocalypse. Jews outside the homeland adapted their worship to their circumstances. If Israel's pre-exile religion elided membership in one kingdom under God with belonging to that deity's devotees, the diaspora severed their civil and religious identities, since many Jews praised the Lord in domains that were distant from the cultic center, ruled by Gentiles, and dominated by an alien culture. Such pluralism nevertheless paralleled a shared distinctiveness that Jews had constructed around the Temple's sanctity, the Torah's influence, the myth of common patriarchal ancestry, and their covenant with God. Critics might charge that priests had profaned the cult, but they did not challenge the Temple's significance.

The appeals that Pharisees, Sadducees, and Essenes made to scripture crossed interpretive swords, but nevertheless elevated the text's importance as a source of religious authority. The toppling of the Second Temple, which removed Judaism's institutional anchor and unmoored Jews from *Eretz Yisrael* even further, ushered in greater changes. It also coincided with the birth of another sect. *Am Yisrael* claimed that the Lord governs all nations while ruling them each under unique terms, heralding the universal God in particularistic terms. Space remained, however, for proclaiming the One God in a less ethnically specific accent. The pronouncement of that gospel also sounded from within the Jewish matrix.

Chapter 2
Jews, Gentiles, and Christians (200 BCE–200 CE)

Christianity arose within the context of Second Temple Judaism: Jesus might be best understood as an itinerant preacher within Jewish apocalyptic tradition and Christianity as initially a Jewish sect. But it soon became something else, attracting Gentiles while absorbing influences from the peoples it encountered. This intercultural dynamic is revealed in the writings that became Christians' holy texts and in their efforts to simultaneously recruit and differentiate themselves from Jews, who "desire signs," and "Greeks," who "desire wisdom" (1 Cor. 1:22).

Jesus of Nazareth (ca. 4 BCE–ca. 30 CE)

"Who do you say that I am?" This deceptively simple question, which Jesus of Nazareth asked his disciples at Caesarea Philippi (Mark 8:29; Matt. 16:15), has elicited complex responses, both historical and theological. The quest for the historical Jesus, begun during the Enlightenment to purge the Gospels of "superstition" by subjecting them to critical reason, has since sought to situate him within his own time and place. That endeavor has proved troublesome. Historians depend on records, the best of which are produced contemporaneously with the events they relate, but most documentation about Jesus is neither collateral nor detailed. Although the Gospels offer abundant information and appear to contain primary-source material, they are not firsthand testimonies, and determining to what degree they may include unmediated reports about Jesus has generated substantial disagreement.

One school of biblical scholars—called "form critics"—regard the Gospels as discrete literary units embedding oral traditions about Jesus that the early Church consolidated for self-justifying (apologetic) purposes; they deny that the Gospels harbor any immediate witness of him. Other theorists hold that a reader can identify such statements by applying prescribed criteria, like independent corroborations of a particular account. The more criteria a passage satisfies, the greater the likelihood it reflects what Jesus actually said and did. Researchers using social memory theory contend that recollection is a cooperative enterprise inflected by events, cultural habits, and constant reinterpretation. Maintaining that the Gospel traditions about Jesus represent residues of communal remembrances, they express skepticism about the odds of discovering authentic material behind the texts. Granting that all historical judgments depend on interpreting sources, and that definitively attributing any word or deed to Jesus is impossible, one might still allow that subjecting the text to differential criteria is a valid means for testing hypotheses about him, while acknowledging that any results are merely probable, rather than certain.

Accepting that the Gospels are problematic sources, we can still sketch Jesus's life and teachings. The evidence puts him among the Jewish peasantry of first-century Palestine. He was born ca. 4 BCE, more likely in or around Nazareth than in Bethlehem, given both widespread doubts about the historicity of Matthew's and Luke's Nativity narratives and recognition of their apologetic aims. He came from a family of modest means, spoke Aramaic, and worked as a carpenter or builder. At about age thirty, he was baptized by an itinerant preacher named John, after which he spent one (or more) years in the Galilee, gaining disciples and sometimes teaching in synagogues. By all accounts he moved easily among and displayed great compassion for people at society's margins. He fomented a major disturbance in Jerusalem, for which he was executed. Some of what Jesus taught was already familiar—the Golden Rule (Matt. 7:12) parallels a saying of the Jewish sage Hillel, his elder contemporary—but much represented a distinctive message about "the kingdom of God," a highly disputed term that many researchers understand as a place and time to come in which God will reign supreme. Heavenly or earthly, future or present, the kingdom would be ushered in by the "Son of Man," an apocalyptic figure whom Jesus may—or may not—have identified as himself. The kingdom's advent is imminent and would occasion a catastrophe, leading to a universal judgment of each person's fitness to enter it that would radically remake the social order. Mark 1:15 offers a concise precis: "'The time is fulfilled, and the kingdom of God has come near; repent, and believe in the good news.'"

Interpreting the historical Jesus has likewise raised controversies. Theories that he resembles a Greek Cynic philosopher who advocated asceticism or a pagan magician have gained little traction—though the Gospels do strongly attest to his reputation as a healer—nor have those identifying him as a Pharisee or Essene. Reflections about the divides in Second Temple Judaism remind us to consider his religious and political milieu. Deeply knowledgeable about Jewish practice and tradition, Jesus in the Gospels assumes a prophetic posture, predicting the Temple's demise while critiquing overscrupulous observance. His concern for society's outcasts and his portrayals of the transformation wrought by the kingdom of God have helped cast him as a militant revolutionary, but he lived a generation before the Zealots, and his admonition that all who take the sword will "'perish'" by it (Matt. 26:52) hardly intimates a rebel chieftain. Self-authorized preachers such as John the Baptist or Theudas, who professed that he could part the Jordan River, roamed first-century Palestine, and Jesus seems to fit this profile. The Jesus Seminar, a group of scholars and laity most active in the 1980s and '90s, represent him as a teacher of wisdom, but other writers regard him primarily as an apocalyptic preacher, which seems more congruent with the Gospels' evidence.

Because of its theological implications and historical ramifications, construing Jesus's death is a hugely contentious exercise. Major shifts in both scholars' appreciation of his Jewishness and the Church's meditation on assigning responsibility for his demise have occurred since the later twentieth century. Jesus sought out the Temple, where his announcements about the kingdom of God and critiques of cultic practice would have maximum impact. He infuriated the high priest and his council (the Sanhedrin), who spurned Jesus's insistence that the kingdom of God was imminent, rejected his censures, and handed him to the Romans. That some Jewish leaders had reasons to rid themselves of a meddlesome prophet is understandable; that all Jews took on that guilt according to Matthew 27:25—an artifact of later Jewish–Christian antagonism—is not. Given the endemic political strains in first-century Judaea, the Romans had their own incentives to silence him, especially during Passover, when hordes of pilgrims intensified Jews' restiveness. Jesus's quick arrest and brutal execution typify Roman reactions to suspected activists; a decade later, they massacred Theudas's supporters and carried his head to Jerusalem. The Romans' view of Jesus as a political risk is manifest by their chosen punishment—crucifixion, a penalty favored for lower-class criminals and insurgents—and by their mocking him as "King of the Jews."

Had events ended there, Jesus might have faded from view, another would-be visionary crying in the wilderness—but they did not. Resurrection beliefs circulated in many Jewish quarters; what Jesus's followers broadcast was the extraordinary witness that he had already risen. For the nascent Jesus movement, their testimonies deflected attention from the message to the man. As a result, what Jesus had said mattered less to his adherents than whom they took him to be: Christos (Greek, "anointed one"), the Messiah.

Introducing Christianity to the Greco-Roman world (ca. 30 CE–ca. 100 CE)

By the mid-first century CE, Jesus's followers had acquired a new name: "Christians" (Acts 11:26). A Latinized Greek word that may be rendered as "Christ-partisans," it was conferred—perhaps by derisive Roman officials—in Antioch, the former Seleucid capital. This provenance is significant, for it suggests how quickly the new movement engaged Gentile populations. At the outset a self-circumscribed group critical of the priesthood but committed to Torah while testifying that Jesus was the risen Messiah, the Jesus movement traversed cultural and religious boundaries with novel speed and design. In the Second Temple's last centuries, Jews accepted converts who satisfied certain ritual obligations, and Judaism attracted "God-fearers," Gentiles who respected some Jewish observances and added the God of Israel to their pantheons.

A few Jews may have considered vigorously converting Gentiles, but such activity—if it occurred—seems to have taken form primarily as literary efforts extolling Judaism's virtues, never as organized recruitment. However much God-fearers may have embraced elements of Judaism, they remained outside Israel's covenant. Jesus's followers, on the contrary, sought to incorporate Gentiles fully into their communities, an endeavor that soon overtook efforts to persuade other Jews of Jesus's messianic nature. How the Jesus movement so quickly acquired its aggressive approach to proselytizing Gentiles is unclear, but it may have resulted from the conclusions that Greek-speaking Jewish followers of Jesus drew after God-fearers in Antioch reacted favorably to their overtures. Whatever the reasons, the Gentile mission took flight immediately, establishing a monumental difference between Jews, who did not evangelize, and Christians, who would be charged to "make disciples of all nations" (Matt. 28:18).

The missionaries entered lands that were politically Roman and culturally Greek. Greco-Roman religious life featured virtually no central structures, creeds, or unique holy places. The only widespread observance was emperor worship, the praxis and meaning of which varied. A plethora of deities ranged from powerful, widely venerated beings (with, for some educated elites, a single high god at the top) to angels who mediated between heaven and earth, domestic spirits that protected the household, and divinized humans. Observances focused on winning the gods' favor to secure a community's welfare, with little consideration given to either moral standards or the afterlife. Individuals seeking to improve their earthly well-being by obtaining arcane religious knowledge could join a mystery cult; those preferring a more rationalist approach might choose a school of philosophy.

These options usually coexisted peacefully, and one might cast off or pick up a god or goddess depending on fortune's twists. Jesus's followers, to the contrary, bore a text-based gospel about the One God who made ethical demands, judged people according to their deeds, and had, in human form, foretold an impending new age. They would confront little opposition from imperial authorities if they raised no political threat, but they also faced disinterest or skepticism from a population inclined to very different religious sensibilities. To make their case required facility in addressing Greco-Roman audiences, so it is unsurprising that the early Church's most successful missionary was such a cultural broker— Paul (born Saul) of Tarsus, a Greek-speaking diaspora Jew, a Pharisee deeply immersed in Torah, and a Roman citizen.

Christianity did not initially triumph in the way Acts implies; in 100 CE, by one estimate, 7,500 believers inhabited an empire of 60 million souls. A minority were "Jewish Christians"—Torah-observant Jews who also recognized Jesus as a messiah—but most were Gentiles, whose acceptance of the new movement required a transcultural leap. Likening Jesus to a demigod or Christianity to a mystery religion may have eased the way for a few, but far more important was Paul's tactic of becoming "all things to all people" (1 Cor. 9:22), adjusting his language to target specific audiences. Couching the news of salvation through faith in the Messiah and the promise of eternal life for the faithful in culturally intelligible terms had persuasive force, as did the missionaries' miraculous powers to heal and converts' opportunities to share Christian communities' spiritual and material resources. Observers from the second-century pagan critic Celsus to Marxist intellectuals have alleged that converts came overwhelmingly from the lower and slave classes, but the first churches in fact attracted individuals from across the social spectrum. Women made up the largest group of converts, perhaps because they gained higher status and power in their families and religious societies than their non-Christian sisters could attain in theirs.

Christianity's penetration of the Greco-Roman world would substantially alter both cultures. Judaism conversed with Hellenism, but Christianity internalized it, perhaps because Christians chose to proselytize on its home ground. Greek, not Aramaic or Hebrew, became the original language of Christian scripture, and Jesus was known universally as *Christos*, not *Mashiach*. Equally important, Christianity engaged with a uniquely Greek epistemology: philosophy. While Greco-Roman religions provided few, if any, ethical guidelines or answers to ultimate questions, philosophers taught their principles to counsel followers on the moral comportment that would lead to personal well-being. Arraying themselves in schools, they touted the superiority of their insights and vied for supporters. Entering this competition, Christianity absorbed some of their teachings to support its emerging theology and practice. From Plato and his disciples, it gained images of God as a perfect unity, good and unchanging, and the human person as an immortal soul housed in a body whose carnal inclinations had constantly to be checked.

From Aristotle, it obtained a logic and metaphysics for understanding the physical universe. More generally, it acquired philosophical habits, learning to present itself systematically through rational argument. By the end of the fifth century CE, Christianity had achieved intellectual respect among the Empire's educated citizenry. An earlier appropriation appears in the Gospel of John: "In the Beginning was the Word, and the Word was with God, and the Word was God" (1:1)—divine thought existing and being actualized in Christ. Neither Genesis nor the Quran construes deific creativity in such a metaphysical cadence.

The New Testament

In form and content, the Christian scriptures cross cultural boundaries. The Jesus movement used Jewish writings as baseline authorities for elaborating the new message in Greek and transmitted it to Gentiles using literary types foreign to contemporary Jewish literature but familiar to Greeks and Romans. Jesus himself had habitually referenced "the law and the prophets" (Matt. 22:40), and his disciples continued the practice, using the Septuagint and other Greek versions of Hebrew texts. Soon, they started citing each other. By 100 CE, a diffuse corpus of writings was circulating, only some of which would become canonical. Eventually, twenty-seven volumes would make up the New Testament, so named because the Septuagint translated "covenant" (*berit*) as "last will" (*diatheke*). The books have come to be arranged roughly by literary genre: gospels, sacred history, correspondence, and apocalypse.

The four Gospels (Old English, "godspel," "good tidings") may resemble ancient biographies formally, but they are ultimately proclamations to follow Jesus Christ as Messiah. Ascribed to Jesus's disciples and their later associates, the Gospels were actually written by anonymous authors who had never met him. Broad consensus exists about their times and places of composition, as well as their probable audiences. Mark came first (ca. 65–ca. 72 CE, addressing Gentile converts outside Palestine); followed by Matthew and Luke (ca. 80–ca. 95 CE, the former pitched to a mixed Jewish- and Gentile-Christian community, the latter to a primarily Gentile one, both outside Palestine); and John (ca. 90–ca. 110 CE, the product of a Jewish-Christian community that began, perhaps, in Judaea). Matthew, Mark, and Luke— known as the "Synoptic" Gospels (literally, texts that are "seen together")—display many similarities, a phenomenon scholars usually explain through the "Four-source hypothesis": Matthew and Luke each used material unique to them, while both also borrowed from Mark and a source known as Q (*Quelle*, German for "source"), a postulated collection of Jesus's sayings thought to have been compiled between 40 and 65 CE.

Although sometimes read as telling essentially the same story with variations in detail, the Synoptics are discrete accounts composed for different communities and conveying disparate perspectives. Mark depicts Jesus as a mysterious figure whose persona his disciples never quite grasp but whom the reader learns is the Son of God, a messiah who—contrary to Jewish expectations of a triumphant king—saves the world through his suffering and death. Matthew emphasizes Jesus's Jewishness to portray a messianic teacher come "not to abolish but fulfill" (5:17) scripture; steeped in Torah, he stresses its ethical demands to the exclusion of ritual, thereby reworking Jewish tradition into a universalized framework that allows Gentiles as well as Jews to participate. Luke downplays Jesus's Jewishness, rendering him primarily as a prophet, born of God, who calls for social justice and preaches about the salvation offered to all. Harnessing different sources and

3. In a late sixteenth-century miniature, St. Matthew writes the Gospel. The image was created by a Hindu painter, likely from a Dutch engraving, for the Muslim Mughal emperor Akbar. Bringing together different religious traditions was typical of Akbar, who promoted his own syncretic religion in an effort to increase toleration among his subjects.

writing in a community that had likely endured bitter separation from neighboring Jews, John characterizes Jesus as a supernatural being, coequal with God, who reveals his identity by performing spectacular miracles and declares that he alone is the way to eternal life.

The New Testament classifies twenty-one books as epistles—personal communications of advice, exhortation, and instruction—although a few do not comfortably fit the form. Seven are grouped as "general" epistles; these are pseudonymous writings, customarily dated to the late first century CE, that deal with pressures on Christian communities and the rifts within them. Usually ordered from 1 Thessalonians (ca. 50 CE) to Romans (ca. 56 CE), the acknowledged Pauline corpus—including 1–2 Corinthians, Galatians, Philippians, and Philemon—is the earliest extant Christian literature. It provided churches struggling to define their beliefs and practices with detailed and innovative theological counsel. The missives did not dwell on Jesus's lessons, but rather on Jesus himself—the risen Messiah whose searing revelation converted Paul from the Church's persecutor into the Gentiles' "apostle" (Rom. 11:13). Human beings are born in thrall to corruption and doomed to die, he taught, but Jesus's sacrifice has made eternal life available as a free gift to all who trust completely in Christ, the resurrected savior who has conquered sin and death. Though he esteemed Jewish tradition and agreed that "the law is holy" (Rom. 7:12), Paul insisted that it was not incumbent on Gentiles, who found salvation by faith in Christ alone. His theological originality, along with his commitments to evangelizing the Gentiles and erecting an ecclesial infrastructure, make it hard to overstate his importance for transfiguring what might otherwise have remained a movement of Jewish reformation into a separate religion.

Acts and Revelation constitute unique genres in the New Testament. The former draws on models from Jewish–Hellenistic historiography, the latter on Jewish apocalyptic literature. Acts was composed as the second volume of Luke's Gospel, but it follows the Gospels and introduces the Epistles, presenting the Church's expansion as fulfilling God's plan. It offers a rationale for evangelization—the end of time has not yet arrived so that missionaries can spread the faith—and certifies the continuity between Jesus (an itinerant preacher with personal disciples) and the institutional apparatus that the next generation is necessarily setting up. It harmonizes the Jewish- and Gentile-Christian missions, asserting the continuing validity of the Jewish scriptures while absolving Gentiles of needing to follow Jewish law.

Revelation was written by John—a prophesier in Asia Minor, not the author(s) of the Johannine gospel and epistles. Whereas Acts' chronological perspective stretches toward an indeterminate horizon, Revelation's posits a looming cataclysm that will end history, inaugurating "a new heaven" and "earth" (21:1). Behind the fantastic imagery of rampaging riders and sadistic locusts lies a historical reality of Roman persecution, perhaps in the mid-60s CE (666, the notorious "number of the beast" [13:19], is usually decoded as "Nero") or the mid-90s. John rages against the "Great Whore of Babylon" (Rome) and implores seven churches in western Asia Minor to keep the faith, for at the end of days, the wicked shall burn in a fiery lake while the righteous will live eternally in a heavenly Jerusalem.

The New Testament offers conflicting perspectives on such matters as the portrayal of Jesus, the timing of his return, and the conduct of missions to Jews and Gentiles, but it also advances some common central principles. The God who works in history has intervened radically by giving divinity human shape in Jesus, the Messiah who offers salvation to all. The Gospels proclaim this good news; the rest of the books rehearse its elaboration and transmission. The New Testament documents the close but tensive relationship between Judaism and the Jesus movement. While incorporating Jewish scriptures, it refigures them to foreshadow Jesus's coming and legitimate his teaching. The New Testament introduces a personal response to God into the covenant and reformulates the figure of the messiah; Jesus is not the Jews' imagined national-liberation leader, but the Word who conquers death. Its sacred history concludes with a cosmic Day of Judgment, not Israel's return to Jerusalem to rebuild the Temple. It invites Gentiles to share in Judaism's ethical monotheism without having to claim a Jewish heritage. Finally, it reveals as well as exemplifies Christians' halting steps toward self-definition.

From sect to church (first and second centuries CE)

The Jesus movement's acceptance of Gentiles, coupled with the refusal of most Jews to convert, facilitated its evolution from a sect within Second Temple Judaism to an independent faith with a rationalized institutional base. Constructing Christian identity involved determining what constituted acceptable beliefs, practices, and sources of religious authority. Building an organization required erecting permanent structures capable of managing expanding networks of churches and settling theological disputes, given the recognition that the end time no longer seemed imminent. During their first two centuries, Christians began to shape their own distinctive religious tradition.

One issue concerned the degree to which Jewish Christians might maintain influence over Christianity as a whole. The Jerusalem community—led by James and Peter, advocates of Christian Torah observance—seemed poised to become the movement's "mother church." Jewish Christians persisted in Palestine and Syria, but their significance waned. Their presence in the Jerusalem church suffered during the Great Revolt, when its members fled before the Temple's demolition, and again after the Romans suppressed a second major uprising—the Bar Kokhba Revolt—in 135 CE, at which point the victors expelled Jews from the city and Gentiles took over the church. Gradually, Jewish Christians' position became untenable: Jews threatened to "put [them] out of the synagogue" for confessing that Jesus is the Messiah (John 9:22), while other Christians suspected them of holding views that were increasingly thought deviant (such as denying the virgin birth). By the mid-second century CE, increasingly self-confident Gentile Christians had marginalized Torah-observant Jesus followers. While retaining some Jewish roots theologically, Christianity had become a Gentile faith in both ethnic and practical terms.

Other disagreements arose about the nature of God and Christ, as well as about which texts and persons should command religious authority. To what degree Christianity may have incorporated a starkly dualistic vision of the universe commonly called "Gnosticism" has stirred substantial scholarly debate; whatever the case, some strands of early Christian thinking refuted Judaism's affirmation of the physical world and asserted that Christ had never taken human form. Such outlooks contended that only those who possessed redemptive *gnosis* (knowledge) of the true God—not the deity whose flawed creation Tanakh celebrates—could escape the material realm of continuous suffering. Marcion, a second-century benefactor of the church in Rome, asserted that Christianity disclosed a previously unknown God of love superior to the Jewish God of law. Parsing Jewish scriptures, he held, was at best irrelevant to, and at worst destructive of, Christian biblical interpretation. He used a prototypical "New Testament" containing versions of a gospel and some Pauline letters to defend his views.

A different sort of challenge emerged in Asia Minor a few decades later, when a movement led by one Montanus came under scrutiny for claiming that adherents—most notoriously women—could speak under the Holy Spirit's direct guidance. "'Hear not me, but hear Christ,'" the prophetess Maximilla claimed—or so alleged a later writer who derided her pretensions to be "the gnosis of persuasion and doctrine." Both Gnostics and Marcionites questioned how much (if any) of the Jewish heritage to retain, while Montanists argued for the capacity of divinely inspired individuals—not just a cadre of elite males—to speak with spiritual authority. All exemplify just how multilateral the first Christian efforts at self-differentiation were.

To some church leaders, however, such diversity represented not acceptable disagreement but fatal error. During the second century CE, figures such as Ignatius, Bishop of Antioch, and Irenaeus, Bishop of Lyons, countered that the Church is "catholic" (Greek *katholike*, "universal"): that is, a unified entity that everywhere preaches a consistent Christian truth. In this context, the term "heresy," which originally and rather innocuously referred simply to a "school of thought," assumed a negative connotation: "poison," as Ignatius put it, contrary to "Christian nourishment." Catholicity catalyzed a centuries-long project to fashion orthodox beliefs and administration. One strategy involved compiling a biblical canon, a definitive list of holy scriptures. Hosts of gospels, acts, epistles, and apocalypses circulated among early Christian communities, as did excerpts from the Septuagint. Marcion's use of a "bible" without the Old Testament is often taken to have spurred canon formation, but the long-term deployment of Christian and Jewish writings to settle theological questions was likely a more important catalyst.

Building consensus about the New Testament's contents took time; by the second century's end, recognition of the four gospels, Paul's epistles, and Acts seems to have been widespread, though not until 367 CE did Athanasius, Bishop of Alexandria, list the exact twenty-seven books now deemed canonical. The Church never achieved such precision with regard to the Old Testament. The core writings remained; Irenaeus voiced the consensus that both testaments exhibit God's Word, the Old previewing what the New exposes. The selection of the Septuagint's additional books varied, with the "deuterocanonical" writings eventually receiving greater esteem in Greek churches than in Latin ones. Irenaeus also helped forge another instrument of uniformity: a creed setting out core principles.

More elaborate formulations would come in the fourth and fifth centuries.

Cultivating unity also depended on regularizing church governance. The initial situation was fluid: settled ministers tended urban house churches while itinerant preachers roamed at will, ecclesiastical officers' duties varied, and local leaders might gain authority through election, charisma, or acts of patronage. Although developments did not proceed evenly, a certain order prevailed by the time of Irenaeus's death. Legitimacy, he declared, belonged only to those officers who had received the true faith preached by Jesus and his disciples—the apostolic tradition— conveyed directly through an unbroken "succession of bishops"— the apostolic succession. Such proclamations put an end to idiosyncratic claims of inspiration through the Spirit; only a representative certified as having received the apostles' license could teach the tradition. Power over Christian communities within each city and its environs fell to the bishop, who ruled a hierarchy of elders and deacons. Having gained leverage to strike at deviance (and deviants), bishops pronounced what was right doctrine and distanced "heretics" from the church. No formal ranking of bishops yet existed, but greater influence accrued to those housed in leading Christian cities, particularly Rome, the Empire's capital and claimed site of its "most ancient church." Still, the bishop of Rome had not yet become the primate (or even "first among equals"); modern references to Roman bishops of this era as "Pope," thereby implying an elevated status, are anachronistic.

By approximately 200 CE, Christian identity was coalescing on three fronts, although the borders erected by partisans on all sides were frequently blurred. Within the Church, a host of institutional and theological issues awaited resolution, but the catholicity project provided both a blueprint for identifying internal aliens, against whom it could construct a Christian identity, and measures for neutralizing them: persuasion, censure, banishment, even magic. The most potent means—namely, state power—came later. Externally, Christians had more or less established that they were not Jews. They did, however, claim to be the new Israel, a universalized update that had entered into a new covenant with God as the Jewish scriptures had forecast. Yet if Christians were no longer Jews, they were not exactly Greeks and certainly not pagans. Exalting one God, they caused disgust and anxiety among pluralists like Celsus, who feared that their exclusivism would upset the Empire's religiously calming multiculturalism. Declaring itself to be something novel, Christianity caught the attention of Jews, who were busily reconstructing Judaism after the Temple's demise, and Romans, who were occupied with maintaining the *Pax Romana*—forcibly, when necessary. The young religion's future would intersect with both.

Chapter 3

Constructing Judaism and Christianity (70 CE–1054 CE)

As Christians labored to fashion their religion and its institutions, Jews faced the task of refashioning theirs. After the Temple's destruction in 70 CE, they had to replace the observances and cult that had depended on its existence, investing legitimacy in new spaces, practices, leaders, and methods of textual interpretation. Christians were similarly trying to systematize their own scriptures, theology, and ecclesiastical organization. These constructions of identity took shape as each group sought to distinguish itself from the other and their political fortunes shifted. Christianity's elevation within the Roman Empire connected the faith to state power in ways that would inform the statement of its core theological premises, amplify divisions within the Church, and configure the course of Jewish–Christian relations.

Rabbinic Judaism (ca. 70 CE–640 CE)

The trauma that Jews endured as a result of Rome's destruction of the Temple would be difficult to overstate. Some Jews fled Judaea, thousands died in captivity or were sold into slavery, many who remained lost their lands, and Rome subjected the province to direct military rule. The religious consequences were more dire still. Emperor Vespasian imposed a "Jewish tax" to rebuild the Temple of Jupiter Capitolinus in Rome, forcing Jews to support a pagan shrine financially. Any hopes they might have entertained about reconstructing their own sanctuary vanished forever after Hadrian's decision in 130 CE to erect an equivalent temple in Jerusalem and his subsequent annihilation of Bar Kokhba's rebellion. Judaism's ritual cornerstone and priesthood were gone, its spatial and liturgical hearts ripped out. Between the Temple's fall and Islam's rise, Jewish communities and a new kind of spiritual leader remade their religion.

A multipurpose, community-based institution, the synagogue (Greek, "assembly"), replaced the Temple as the center of public religious life. Synagogues took on functions previously performed across multiple settings. The earliest archaeological evidence shows Egyptian Jews in the mid-third century BCE congregating in a prayer house. First-century CE Palestinian Jews like Jesus—who expounded the book of Isaiah one "sabbath" in Nazareth (Luke 4:16)—gathered to study scripture. Synagogues also served secular purposes; at least one in Jerusalem included a guest house, perhaps for diaspora pilgrims. By the fourth century CE, synagogues had become venues for worship that included prayer and scripture reading, as well as repositories for Torah scrolls—localized Holies of Holies.

Identifying precisely which books should be considered sacred took a similarly long time. The Torah had likely been compiled by about 400 BCE and the Prophets by about 200 BCE, but these anthologies did not yet comprise a "canon." Between 70 and 150 CE, someone certified that Tanakh contained twenty-four specific books, though questions lingered for another century and the definitive text would not be settled until later in the millennium. Jewish self-definition against pagans and Christians—who were simultaneously beginning their own canonization debates—had something to do with the chronology of the Tanakh's "closing," although the process had begun long before Christianity appeared. More importantly, designating a delimited body of writings as divinely inspired invested them with religious power.

The people largely responsible for reshaping Judaism called themselves "sages," though "rabbi" is now more familiar to us. The term first meant "my master" or "teacher," but, by the third century CE, it designated a class of judges or legal advisers. The rabbinic movement's formation and early trajectory are somewhat obscure. Following the Temple's demise, surviving elites—including former Pharisees, Sadducees, priests, and scribes—organized closed communities on the basis of rules grounded in scriptural study that members hoped to prescribe for all Jews. These gatherings gained status among Jews in Palestine and throughout the diaspora when the Romans, in the late second century, elevated Rabbi Judah ha-Nasi ("the Prince") to the office of Patriarch, a liaison between imperial officials and Palestinian Jewish communities. Judah seems to have sponsored rabbinic activity in his court, a model for later academies in Galilee and Mesopotamia. The rabbis did not create the synagogue, whose practices they sometimes derided, nor did they unilaterally determine the composition of Tanakh, the contents of which reflected a long collective process. They did, however, create a fresh liturgical environment by legitimating new practices, such as communal prayer as a proper means for soliciting divine favor in place of the bygone priestly sacrifices. Such innovations rested on a fundamental assertion: supreme religious authority was vested in the "Torah"—by which they meant far more than the Five Books of Moses—as parsed by the rabbis themselves.

The rabbinic project was grounded in an interpretive claim made explicit by about 300 CE, but operative earlier. The Written Torah, Tanakh, warrants exegesis, which requires not prophetic revelation but, rather, close study of the Oral Torah: the traditions that God taught Moses at Sinai and that were subsequently passed on to the rabbis and their students. Thus accorded equal validity, the Oral Law amplifies and reinterprets the Written Law, tying Tanakh to its rabbinic exegetes. Oral and written components together compose the "dual Torah." The first application of these principles was the compilation of the Mishnah ("Repeated

Tradition"), overseen by Judah ha-Nasi around 200 to 225 CE. Treating such subjects as religious festivals and family life, it elaborates scriptural passages to spell out the proper legal procedure (*halakhah*) for fulfilling God's commandments. For instance, Deuteronomy's laconic charge to "Observe the sabbath" (5:12) discloses, when placed under rabbinic scrutiny, thirty-nine categories of labor that a dutiful observer must shun.

The Mishnah is not case law; it records sundry opinions without necessarily resolving them. To further plumb the Written Torah's depths, rabbis also developed a method, *midrash* ("seeking"), grounded on the presumption that its text is perfect, hence any word or passage can illuminate any other. By extension, *midrash* also references literature using this technique, much of it compilations of *aggadah*—traditions dealing with history, theology, and ethics—germane to one or another volume in Tanakh. The rabbinic project culminated in two collections of the Talmud (Hebrew, "study"), sprawling compendia of *halakhah* and *aggadah* in which layers of annotation engorge the Mishnah and other *midrashic* writings. One version was completed in Palestine by 400 CE and the other (which has assumed greater prominence) in Babylonia around 500 CE. They establish the Torah scroll as the locus of divine writ, while simultaneously granting human commentators wielding the Oral Torah equivalent interpretive authority.

Judaism as it emerged during this time preserved ancient traditions in radically new guises. The Temple remained resonant in memory, but public worship took place in synagogues, decentralized sanctuaries housing the designated corpus of written tradition. Those holy scrolls were themselves subject to interpretation by rabbis who claimed the religious gravitas once enjoyed by priests and prophets. Using the Oral Torah, they built a discipline that converted the Temple's rituals of atonement into a system of *halakhah* in which properly performing life's routines, rather than attending public rites, became the primary instrument for serving God. Most Jews did not accept the rabbis' claims immediately; festooned with figurative art or lacking partitions to segregate women, synagogues sometimes evinced a popular piety that snubbed rabbinic directives. Rabbis did not achieve religious headship within Jewish communities until perhaps the Middle Ages. Nevertheless, they utterly transformed Judaism well before then.

Church(es) and empire(s) (64 CE–600 CE)

The rabbinic movement proceeded without much Roman notice; as Jewish political agitation subsided, Roman policy softened, leaving Jews voluntarily isolated from the state's daily oversight. Christians did feel Roman pressure, albeit not quite as heavily or consistently as martyrs' legends may suggest. Between the reigns of emperors Nero (r. 54–68) and Decius (r. 249–251), persecution was typically sporadic and local, initiated mainly by provincial officials responding to popular allegations that Christian worship featured cannibalism and incest. Religious anxieties twitched political nerves; to Roman sensibilities, Christians' recognition of the One God both affronted their own gods and subverted the polity whose stability depended on those deities' beneficence.

These concerns escalated as barbarians crowded the borders, confidence in the gods slumped, and the percentage of Christians within the Empire quintupled between 250 and 300. By then, orders to restrict their behavior issued from the top. The worst came under Diocletian (r. 284–305), who decreed that Christians' scriptures be confiscated, their churches destroyed, and their clergy imprisoned. During the "Great Persecution" (303–311), Christians suffered imprisonment, slavery, and death. We cannot gauge numbers; the tally of forty-seven executions that the church historian Eusebius of Caesaria (fl. 290–335) recorded in Palestine suggests a scale of mortality but not of terror. In North Africa, one of the areas hardest hit, persecution caused deep divisions among Christians about whether those who had recanted under pressure should be allowed to re-enter the Church. It also fostered a cult of martyrs.

As the Great Persecution wound down, Christians experienced a stunning reversal of fortune. Diocletian had split the Empire into eastern and western halves, with senior and junior rulers. Designed to lessen the risk of civil war, his reform instead precipitated one. Constantine, the Augustus (senior ruler) of the western portion, was determined to rule the entire empire himself. He attributed an important victory over a rival claimant to divine intervention, although Eusebius's depiction of him beholding a celestial cross of light inscribed "'By this conquer'" is likely highly exaggerated. However Christian (or pagan) his vision may have been, Constantine thereafter changed the Empire's posture toward the Church from tormentor to supporter. He concurred in issuing the Edict of Milan (313), which granted toleration to all religious groups (including Christians), gave bishops judicial power, and funded a massive campaign of church-building in places such as Rome, Constantinople (his designated capital), and Jerusalem—thus initiating its makeover from Roman colony to Christian holy site and influential see (a bishop's jurisdiction). Most momentously, he mobilized state power behind efforts to unify the Church and inserted himself into theological controversies. Only one subsequent emperor would pursue an anti-Christian policy, and in 380, an edict established Nicene Christianity as the Empire's official religion, aligning state power behind this particular definition of orthodoxy and outlawing the imperial cult.

As the Empire sanctioned the Church, the Church found itself increasingly affected by changing conditions within the Empire. Linguistic differences between Christians in the West and East opened in the second and third centuries, when Roman bishops began writing in Latin rather than Greek, increasing the possibility for theological misunderstandings. Politics amplified this divide. The boundaries of Diocletian's reorganization more or less separated Latin- from Greek-speaking realms. The subsequent fates of the Empire's western and eastern halves altered the Church's political contexts. Rome fell in 476, and the western empire dissolved, replaced by an array of smaller polities. The eastern empire, centered in Constantinople, adopted its capital's old name (Byzantion), identified itself as Roman even as it spoke Greek, and reached its greatest extent under Justinian I (r. 527–565). Born into a single state, Christianity had come to inhabit different sociopolitical contexts. In the fragmented West, the Church often functioned as the civil order and operated independently of much state supervision; in the East, emperors continued to regulate the Church. These conditions influenced how church leaders dealt with competing claims about the nature of God and the sites of ecclesiastical authority. They also provided a backdrop for Christians' relationships with Jews.

The nature(s) of God and Christ (100 CE–640 CE)

Arguably the most vexing theological conundrums the Church has ever faced concerned the nature(s) of Christ and the Godhead. Christians inherited Jewish conceptions of the One God who was unchanging and ineffable, yet showed emotion and intervened in the world. Jews might disregard those inconsistencies, but Christians—who proclaimed that Jesus was the Son of God incarnate (made flesh) while juggling philosophical conceptions of God's immutability—could not. If Jesus had been born of both the Holy Spirit and a woman, was he human, divine, or both—and, if both, how? That query forced another: did his (and the Spirit's) perceived autonomy compromise God's axiomatic unity? How could three individuals compose one God? Working out the answers occupied Christians for centuries, since the issues—theological and political—were complex and intertwined.

Some early positions reduced Jesus to a fully human messiah, or conversely, a being whose earthly body was mere illusion. By 300, certain broad concepts had gained traction. Jesus Christ was a single "person" composed of both human and divine "substances"; the Godhead consisted of three figures unified—a Trinity. No firm consensus prevailed, however, and the nuances that theologians infused into such technical terms as "person" and "substance" did not always translate smoothly between Latin and Greek, breeding confusion and mistrust. Early in the fourth century, Arius, an Alexandrian church elder, proposed that the Son is a human body in which divine reason replaced the rational soul. Infuriated by his subordination of the Son, an Egyptian synod exiled Arius, but local assemblies could not legislate for the entire Church. Constantine solved that problem. Having unified his empire in 324, he determined to unite the Church, convening an ecumenical council of bishops at Nicaea the next year. It pronounced Father and Son "consubstantial" (*homoousion*) and deployed language—"very God of very God," "begotten, not made"—denying Arian claims.

Theologians reconsidered this settlement for more than fifty years. To avoid collapsing Father and Son into a monad, a "semi-Arian" party advocated *homoiousion*—they are of "like" substance. Contrarily, Apollinaris, a Syrian bishop, exalted Christ's divinity, insisting that he had a body and soul, but was not a human being. Meanwhile, a few church leaders refused to admit the Spirit's divinity. Concerned, like Constantine, that partisan brawls might unsettle the Empire, Emperor Theodosius I convened another ecumenical council at Constantinople in 381. Its settlement owed much to the three "Cappadocian Fathers," who produced a compromise as much linguistic as theological. They redefined key terms to conceive each person in the Trinity as distinct equals— not a monad—who nevertheless shared a single underlying substance, making them one God, not three. The Council revised what now became known as the Nicene–Constantinopolitan Creed, underlining, for instance, that Jesus Christ was begotten from the Father "before all ages."

Constantinople largely resolved the Trinitarian issues, but left open the Christological ones, which overlay a disagreement between Alexandria and Antioch. The former emphasized the divinity of God made flesh, the latter the humanity of Jesus who is also Christ. Tempers erupted when Nestorius, a bishop trained in Antioch, argued that, since Christ's two natures did not unite completely, Mary was Mother of Christ (*Christotokos*) but not Mother of God (*Theotokos*). Cyril, Bishop of Alexandria, retorted that the eternal Word had joined with flesh in her womb; although Christ came *from* two natures, he was one person with one (composite) nature formed by the joining of his divine and human elements. Mary was *Theotokos* indeed. After decades of recriminations, excommunications, compromise formulations, and a last effort by the Alexandrians to force one-nature language, Emperor Marcian convened the Council of Chalcedon in 451. Favoring Antiochene sentiment while also acknowledging Cyril, it declared that Jesus was one person and substance begotten *in* "two natures," their different properties "preserved" by the union, not extinguished. The vast majority of Christians did—and do—accept this formulation.

But not all of them. Passions continued to run high. Of the eight patriarchs (highest ranking bishops), both pro- and anti-Chalcedon, appointed in Alexandria during the four decades following the council, four were expelled by one side or the other, and one was murdered. Two groups rejected the settlement. Miaphysites—who favored a one-nature (*mia physis*) solution—expounded Cyril's position. Chalcedonian bishops harassed and even executed them when they could. Seeking political stability, Byzantine emperors alternately accommodated or suppressed them. Justinian tried both tactics, deposing Miaphysites from their sees even as his wife, Empress Theodora, accorded them refuge. By the 540s, Miaphysites were erecting an alternative structure whose legacy, the "Oriental Orthodox Churches," survives in Egypt, Syria, Armenia, and Ethiopia. A second party subscribed to the two-nature (*dyo physis*) theory of Nestorius. Persecuted by the Byzantine Empire and reviled by Miaphysites, they fled to eastern Syria, Mesopotamia, and Persia, reaching

India and China. The "Church of the East" never secured a ruler's patronage, however, and its adherents wound up as small minorities, often in Muslim lands. The Assyrian Church of modern Iraq and Syria is one example.

These disputations might strike even a sympathetic modern observer as overwrought, and an unsympathetic one as manifestly absurd, but behind the intellectual and political gymnastics lay profound religious stakes. The proclamation that God had come to earth was fundamental to the machinery of Christian redemption. Jesus had taken human form and died for humanity's sins; if he had not, two-nature proponents feared, he could not redeem humanity. For one-nature adherents, however, danger lurked in exalting Jesus's humanity, for anything less than asserting Christ's full divinity negated his power to save. Moreover, worshipping a human being constituted idolatry. Free to build redemption theories without Jesus, Jews and Muslims assume that stance. But for Christians, the Incarnation's marvelousness and the Trinity's mystery afford a unique and profound perspective on how the One God loves the world. Setting out the "right" path to salvation was well worth the turmoil.

Constantinople and Rome (451–1054)

The Council of Chalcedon recognized Rome, Constantinople, Alexandria, Antioch, and Jerusalem as the five paramount sees. Their struggles for power and influence devolved into a long contest between the first two. Rome took pride in vigorously defending the Chalcedonian Creed. Although they generally upheld it, Byzantines disposed to reconciling with Miaphysites did not always pay the papacy homage. When Emperor Zeno proposed an accommodation with the Miaphysites that offended Roman sensibilities, Pope Felix III excommunicated the Patriarch of Constantinople, precipitating a schism (484–519) that mended only after Emperor Justin I, eager to conciliate the papacy to further his imperial ambitions, accepted a formula affirming

Rome's primacy. Hoping to mollify Miaphysites by condemning the writings of three theologians whom Chalcedon had declared to be acceptable, Justinian coerced approval from Pope Vigilius by essentially keeping him under house arrest in Constantinople for seven years. These rows portended future strains.

The authority of Constantinople's patriarch reflected the city's importance as hub of the most dominant Eastern Christian tradition, especially as Antioch, Alexandria, and Jerusalem fell to Muslim armies in the seventh century. Byzantine religion developed around certain emphases, including a role for the emperor that was both powerful and ritually dramatic. Ranked in an ecclesiastical hierarchy below only God and the angels, he could depose clergy and intervene in theological controversies, but could not set doctrine unilaterally. He also anchored citywide Eucharistic processions to Hagia Sofia, a public rite that was simultaneously civic and religious. Another trait was concern for right doctrine. The Byzantine Church upheld Chalcedon, although only after a third ecumenical council in Constantinople (680–681) condemned two final efforts to compromise with the Miaphysites.

Paradoxically, this concern for orthodoxy fostered a devotional culture rooted not in pursuit of doctrinal knowledge, but rather in a spirituality that emphasized humanity's intimacy with God, the theological backbone for which was *theosis*, "deification." As expounded by Maximus the Confessor, a seventh-century theologian and mystic, the communication of God's grace into an individual's soul and body—a phenomenon modeled by Jesus Christ's deified humanity—both makes one more authentically human and draws one closer to God. This synergy between God's energy and human action does not literally make a person divine, but it does allow one to live fully in Christ's being. The logic of *theosis* encouraged decorating the walls of Orthodox churches with images of the Holy Family and the saints that reflected cosmic hierarchies while reminding congregants of their constant proximity to the divine. The Byzantine tradition outlived the

4. Hagia Sophia, the "Great Church" of the Byzantine Empire and a
model for Muslim religious architecture, in use as a mosque during the
mid-nineteenth century. Its mosaics of Christian and Byzantine
imperial figures—plastered over in this view—were uncovered when
the Turkish Republic converted it into a museum in the twentieth
century.

Empire, its theology and liturgy passing into the modern self-headed Orthodox churches in Russia, eastern Europe, and Turkey.

A struggle over iconoclasm (the destruction of religious images) ultimately solidified art's importance as a means for increasing communication between human beings and the divine. In the late seventh century, anxieties stoked by the Empire's contracting borders and recognition of Islam's growing prominence encouraged beliefs that pictures of the Holy Family and the saints gave access to spiritual power, but revering icons raised concerns about idolatry. A recurring backlash climaxed in 754, when a synod condemned representations of Christ: since images could portray only his human side, the synod reasoned, they heretically divided his two natures. Hoping to reunify the church, Empress Irene called the seventh ecumenical council (Nicaea, 787), which reversed this judgment, warning that to reject Christ's physical appearance denied the Incarnation. Anti-image forces gained power once again until another synod, called by Empress Theodora, affirmed Nicaea's stand. The initial observance of the Iconoclasts' defeat—which was celebrated in Hagia Sophia on the first Sunday of Lent in 843—has since become a major feast—the Triumph of Orthodoxy—in the Eastern Churches' liturgical calendar. Much about the controversy remains unresolved, but it unarguably secured icons as an enduring element of Orthodox devotion.

The papacy approved Second Nicaea's decision on images, but strains between the eastern and western churches continued. Two issues proved especially trying. Although the Nicene–Constantinopolitan Creed stated that the Holy Spirit proceeds only from God the Father, Latin churches began to add the word *Filioque* ("and from the Son") during mass. Rome adopted the clause formally in 1014, but Constantinople refused. More corrosive was the papacy's continued assertion of primacy in the face of the patriarchate's claim of equality. Tension resurfaced in 1054, when Pope Leo IX solicited Byzantine aid against Norman invaders. Deeming *Filioque* an untoward innovation, claims of papal supremacy baseless, and the Latin custom of celebrating the Eucharist with unleavened bread both Jewish in practice and heterodox in theology, Patriarch Michael Cerularius opposed an alliance. After months of mutual snubs and reproaches, the papal legate slapped a bull of excommunication on Hagia Sophia's altar just before the liturgy; an Orthodox synod quickly reciprocated. The mutual anathemas were personal, not corporate, and what has subsequently been called the "Great Schism" did not immediately sever official relations. Nevertheless, the rift never healed, and the Fourth Crusade's conquest of Byzantium in 1204 worsened matters. The Catholic and Orthodox Churches rescinded the excommunications only in 1965 and are still not officially reconciled, although negotiations continue. The events of 1054 represented another insult to the notion that all Christians belonged to a universal community. Disputes over God's nature and who should lead the Church had sundered the ideal of a unified body of Christ into a host of competing organs.

Early Jewish–Christian relationships (30–640)

The earliest Jewish–Christian relationships developed within the Roman imperial context. During their first three centuries of coexistence, Jews and Christians were minority communities tolerated as imperial authorities saw fit. Romans often derided Jews for their distinctive customs, and the state crushed their rebellions. At the same time, some Romans admired Jews' ethics and belief in one God, accorded Judaism respect for its antiquity, and considered it a taproot of Greek philosophy, making Plato, according to one second-century thinker, "but Moses speaking Attic Greek." The Empire regarded Judaism as a legitimate religion, gave Jews the unique privilege of not having to appease pagan gods, and inadvertently boosted the rabbinic movement by installing Judah ha-Nasi as patriarch. Christianity, on the other hand, looked to Romans like a superstition, a potentially dangerous novelty unsanctioned by ancient heritage. It was, therefore, illicit, and Christians could face persecution on grounds of refusing to worship the pagan deities. To counter such charges, apologists such as Justin Martyr and Origen asserted that Christianity derived from the Abrahamic and Mosaic sources that fed into Hellenic wisdom.

Such arguments did not identify Christianity with Judaism; indeed, they helped articulate Christians' distinctiveness, to both Romans and Christians. One popular model explicating how and why the Jesus movement became Christianity as distinct from Judaism represents them as two roads diverging from a common path that ran through Second Temple Judaism. This "parting of the ways" has raised criticism for treating Judaism and Christianity as monoliths and for neglecting subsequent contacts between Jews and Christians (as well as pagans and, eventually, Muslims). Some measure of intellectual contact continued, both directly (Origen learned Hebrew from Jewish tutors) and indirectly (rabbis and church leaders monitored each other's debates). Cultural and religious mingling likewise persisted, albeit decried by boundary guardians on both sides: rabbis who disapproved of the Dura Europos synagogue's painting of pharaoh's daughter bathing naked matched John Chrysostom's screeds against Christians who visited synagogues. Neither saint nor rabbi would have approved of how Jews, Christians, and pagans, each venerating Abraham in their own way, mixed at a fair in fourth-century Mamre—traditionally the site where Abraham settled. Still, it is hard to know how frequently such encounters occurred and how much one can extrapolate from them. The most clear-cut parting involved Jewish Christians, whose separation from Jews was well underway by 100 CE and whose division from Gentile Christians (who came to consider them heretics) accelerated later on.

The theological distancing is easier to plot. On the Christian side, a rhetoric known as *Adversus Judaeos* ("Against the Jews") had materialized by the mid-second century, expounded by apologists who struck certain themes. Jews misconstrue their own scriptures, they claimed, whereas Christians, who read the Old Testament allegorically instead of literally, interpret them correctly. Jews rejected and killed Jesus, and their subsequent misfortunes demonstrate God's just punishment. Written not to engage Jews but to structure an orthodox Christian theology, this literature allowed the Church to call itself the new Israel without having to accept "un-Christian" practices and to advertise that it had superseded the old Israel, which survived only to highlight Christian truth. As Augustine of Hippo, one of the Church's most preeminent theologians, argued, Jews should be spared because their ongoing humiliation testified to the verity of the scriptures and of Christ Messiah. *Adversus Judaeos* built a robust Christian identity on a framework that simultaneously valued and denigrated Judaism. This tension has resurfaced throughout Christian history as a nagging concern about "Judaizing," the charge that some group's practices are too "Jewish," hence heretical. Formulating the Trinity defined Christianity from within; differentiating itself from Judaism framed it from without.

By contrast, rabbinic Judaism's central texts virtually ignore Christianity, partly for reasons of chronology and geography. The Mishnah and the Palestinian Talmud were completed before Christian rulers escalated the persecution of Jews, and the Babylonian Talmud was compiled under the Zoroastrian Sasanid empire (224–651), where Christians were themselves a minority whom Jews did not need to rebut. More importantly, the rabbinic movement on the whole did not deploy "heresy" and "orthodoxy" as central categories for Jewish self-definition. One rabbi told his students that the persons of the Trinity "are three titles for a single Being," but such mentions are tiny droplets in a vast textual sea. Jesus figures not as a frequent theological subject but an occasional polemical object, derided for his illegitimate birth, feats of magic, and outlandish claims to divinity. The Talmuds classify non-Jewish cults under a variety of technical terms but accord Christianity little notice. Much debate has surrounded the *birkat ha-minim* ("the benediction [of God] on heretics"), a prayer extant by perhaps the late first century CE, which in different versions invokes divine destruction on groups ambiguously defined. The opinion that it aimed at all Christians and helped precipitate the "parting" has fallen from favor; more probably, it initially targeted Jewish Christians. Jewish identity was constructed much less by opposition to Christianity than by internal forces.

Only in the fourth century, according to some scholars, should we speak of Judaism and Christianity as separate entities, at least in the sense of their possessing determined theological boundaries. By then, the *birkat ha-minim* may have targeted Gentile Christians too, a reflection of Jews' declining status in Roman lands as Christianity gained political purchase. Its proclamation as the Empire's official religion demoted Jews to second-class citizenship. Between 388 and 438, imperial actions prohibited them from marrying Christians, forbade them from joining the armed forces, abolished the long-standing Galilean patriarchy, and excluded them from public office. In 553, Justinian took the unprecedented step of interfering with the liturgy, barring rabbinic biblical interpretations from the service. The stage was set for more than a millennium of Jewish dispossession in Christianized Europe, although Jews would usually escape persecution as heretics, their allowance sanctioned by arguments like Augustine's.

The dynamics by which Christians and Jews had defined themselves in opposition to one another would soon be complicated by a phenomenon emerging from lands beyond Christian control. Claiming that they, too, were Abraham's descendants, its adherents would change political currents far beyond the Levant. As they did, they inherited a Christian conundrum about the Jews that now applied to Christians too—how to treat people who were not quite heretics, nor true believers. That phenomenon was Islam.

Chapter 4
Islam: Religion, politics, and the state (600–1258)

Islam arose in an area contested by competing empires and populated by diverse religious groups. Muhammad's revelations, recorded in the Quran, drew loosely on Jewish and Christian ideas, but they pointedly situated him within the biblical prophetic tradition. Muslims asserted that they had recovered the original religion of Abraham. At its inception, the Muslim religious community, or *umma*, was also a political body, but the problems inherent in investing spiritual and civil headship in one person manifested themselves quickly. Clashes about who should guide the *umma* inflected Islamic religious identity, deeply influencing its eventual division into two major sects.

Muhammad and his milieu (ca. 570–632 CE)

Like ancient Israel and Roman Judaea, seventh-century Arabia was not a prominent economic, political, or cultural center, but its wider connections helped make it the locus of a major religious movement. Throughout much of the peninsula, nomads exchanged animal products for dates and wheat grown around oases such as Yathrib and Mecca. Localized tribes, not centralized states, formed the basic political organizations. Indigenous religious life before the rise of Islam is hard to reconstruct, since Muslim polemic, which portrays the pre-Islamic era as *jahiliyya*, a barbarous "time of ignorance," colors most of the sources. Cultic practice included worshipping idols, stars, and rocks, which were often surrounded by sacred precincts to which tribes made pilgrimages—notably, the Kaba, a cubic building in Mecca containing a black meteoric stone. Such sanctuaries could also serve as market centers for caravans. Arabs recognized multiple deities and spirits (*jinn*) but, like Greek and Roman polytheists, regarded them as potential benefactors rather than moral authorities. Even prominent divinities—such as Allah (*al-Ilah*, "the God"), considered by many Arabs at the time to be the creator deity—likely had little cultic importance. Other religions had made inroads via trading contacts, migrations, missions, and the maneuverings between the Sasanid Persian and the Roman (later Byzantine) empires. These incursions pulled Arabs into the region's wider religious and political developments.

Judaism and Christianity enjoyed more exposure than did other imports, such as Manichaeism and Zoroastrianism. By the fifth and sixth centuries, Jewish tribes inhabited western Arabian oases. Nestorian Christians fled Byzantine orthodoxy for Mesopotamia, while Miaphysites moved into the northern Syrian desert and southern Arabia. The question of what Muhammad's revelations (and Islam more generally) may have owed to Jewish and Christian influence is a highly sensitive issue with seventh-century roots. The Quran identifies Abraham as a *hanif,* an "upright" individual who rejected idolatry and submitted fully to Allah. It repudiates Arab polytheism while contending that this "[true] religion" (*hanifiyya,* Qur. 3:19) preceded Judaism and Christianity and owes them essentially nothing. These claims run parallel to arguments that Islam is a product more particularly of Arabia than of the greater Middle East.

Yet, although some scholars allow for the possibility that the term *hanifiyya* points to the existence of a real (if elusive) phenomenon, others believe that it demonstrates little more than an effort by early Muslims to distinguish their monotheism from already existing ones. Whatever the case, Muhammad's invocations of Abraham and the prophetic tradition from Adam to Jesus presume some acquaintance with Judaism and Christianity, and the Quran's references to *Tawrat* and *Injil* presuppose awareness of other scriptures. By Muhammad's time, a diffuse "ethical prophetic monotheism" had suffused the Eastern Mediterranean, provoking contests between Jews and Christians over who constituted Abraham's true descendants. The Quran's concerns were hardly unique, and Islam was not just a product of Arabia. Nevertheless, distinctively Arabian aspects of early Islamic practice are easy to find, beginning with the ritual of pilgrims circling around the Kaba. It is difficult to match Quranic statements with precise biblical antecedents, and reductionist to cast Islam as merely redacting or revising its predecessors. The Quran draws upon a regional storehouse of common religious knowledge—stories about Abraham and Jesus, discussions about the extent of God's oneness and justice—to serve its own ends.

According to the traditional narrative, Muhammad was born around 570 into a clan of the Quraysh, the tribe that controlled access to the Kaba. Orphaned at a young age, he gained protection from an uncle and entered commerce in the employ of Khadija, an older woman whom he then married. Having received his first revelation from the angel Gabriel in 610, he soon began preaching submission (*islam*) to the One God, hatred of idol-worship, the necessity of repentance, and belief in an impending final judgment. These messages challenged both Meccans' religious sensibilities and their profits from pilgrims. Facing ridicule and threats, he experienced profound authentication of his prophetic call during the Night Journey, in which he miraculously traveled from Mecca to Jerusalem, praying with Abraham, Moses, and Jesus before ascending to the highest heaven. Left politically vulnerable by the deaths of his uncle and wife, he and some supporters ("Emigrants") escaped in 622 to Yathrib (subsequently renamed Medina, the "City [of the Prophet]"). The migration's date begins the Islamic calendar.

Invited by Medinans to adjudicate their disputes, he joined the Emigrants and local "Helpers" into the *umma* while regarding Jewish tribes as equal—"the Jews have their religion and the Muslims have theirs"—a status contingent on their remaining loyal allies. This arrangement soon soured, however, as most Jews rejected Muhammad's prophetic claims, and some were implicated in supporting the Meccans, leading to the expulsion of two tribes, the enslavement and execution of a third, and the reformulation of rites suddenly deemed too "Jewish," such as changing the direction Muslims faced while praying from Jerusalem to Mecca. Meanwhile, the revelations persisted, now concerned principally with establishing a just social order within an *umma* increasingly defined in exclusively Muslim terms. Muhammad eventually prevailed over the Meccans militarily, diplomatically, and spiritually. Having already redefined the Kaba as a pilgrimage site by destroying its idols, he undertook the first Muslim *hajj* (pilgrimage) in 632. Later that year he died of illness in Medina.

Non-Muslim scholars have challenged this account, questioning the reliability of its sources. It depends substantially on *sira*s ("lives") of the Prophet, a genre methodologically closer to modern biography than the Gospels are, but chronologically more distant from its subject than they are. Ibn Ishaq composed the earliest, most authoritative example more than a century after Muhammad's death, and it survives only in critical editions revised generations later still. Ishaq drew heavily on reports (*hadith*) about the Prophet's words and deeds said to have been passed down from his closest associates, the Companions. This process, like the formation of the apostolic succession within the Church, institutionalized a chain of religious authority stretching back to the tradition's founding figure. Profuse, fragmented, and contradictory, the *hadith* have elicited further skepticism because of their murky provenance. In the ninth and tenth centuries, Muslim scholars assembled chains of transmission to verify which items could be traced to the Companions without interruption, but though the most trusted collections are foundational for Islamic law, few historians believe that they contain much genuine evidence. Contemporary non-Muslim sources confirm only scattered details about Muhammad, and the single seventh-century Islamic witness—the Quran—is not (nor does it purport to be) a biography. The historical quests for both Muhammad and Jesus thus face similar dilemmas.

The Quran (610–900)

The Quran's relationship to Tanakh and the Bible differs from that of the New Testament to Tanakh. Whereas the New Testament reinterprets Tanakh and incorporates it into the Bible as the Old Testament, the Quran refers to the Jewish and Christian scriptures while remaining independent of both. It mentions prophets repeatedly while overlooking Isaiah, for instance, and it grants Mary greater coverage than does the New Testament while omitting Paul entirely. It retells biblical incidents in original ways. These contrasts reflect the historical and cultural distance between first-century Palestine and seventh-century Arabia. Unlike Jesus, who preached from within a highly elaborated religious structure, Muhammad developed an emergent monotheism in a decentralized spiritual terrain where Jews and Christians were thin on the ground. Likely illiterate, he inhabited an oral culture accustomed to creating and communicating texts vocally, rather than transmitting and interpreting them literarily. The Quran draws allusively, rather than methodically, on Jewish and Christian materials circulating by word of mouth, including stories from Jewish tradition, apocryphal gospels, and folklore. Such sources, called the *Israiliyyat* ("Israelite tales"), had a deep impact on early Islamic literature and exegesis.

The Quran departs from Tanakh and the Bible in both format and literary structure. It is a single volume composed of what might be described as oral poetry that embeds snippets of stories, parables, liturgies, and laws. The text is broken into 114 *suras*

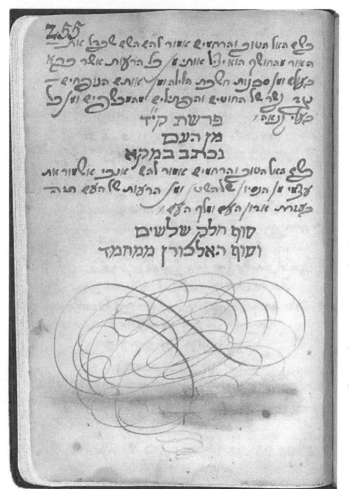

5. The last page of a Quran that was written primarily in a semicursive Ashkenazic Hebrew script. It forms the greatest part of a manuscript that also includes an essay on Muslim customs and a short biography of Muhammad, all meant to inform the Jewish community of mid-eighteenth-century Cochin, India, about their Muslim neighbors. The translator—a Jewish convert to Christianity—worked from a Dutch-language text, itself a translation from a French rendering of the Arabic.

(conventionally called "chapters") that are generally arranged in descending order of length. Each now bears a number (adopted from Western practice) and a name added later by Muslims. Tradition has assigned some to the Meccan period and others to the Medinan. A number are composites, hence difficult to date confidently. All but one begin with a formula, the *Bismillah*: "In the Name of God, the Merciful, the Compassionate." *Suras* were separated quite early into *ayas* ("signs," or symbols of fundamental truth); each "verse" represents itself as a unit of revelation. Different versions of the Quran may show slight variations in the *ayas*' identification and numbering (another borrowed usage). Its authorial voice belongs not to a person, as in the prophetic books or the Gospels' quotations from Jesus, but to God; Muhammad merely channels divine speech. No chronological, narrative, or expository framework organizes matter between *suras* or (with a few exceptions) within them. The Quran collates self-contained, narratively unconnected prophecies.

Unlike Tanakh and the New Testament, the Quran did not undergo a canonization process, but it did endure complicated redactions involving the establishment of the consonantal text and its vocalization. The most dominant Muslim tradition relates that Muhammad's listeners inscribed individual prophecies on physical objects (such as palm leaves and animal bones) and in memory, collections eventually passed to Uthman bin Affan (r. 644–656), the third caliph. He appointed a commission to produce a codex, distributed it, and ordered all other versions burned. Variant tellings contradict this story; some credit the collection to Abu Bakr, the first caliph (r. 632–634), and others to Umar ibn al-Khattab, the second caliph (r. 634–644). Western scholarship has logged additional criticisms. The earliest physical evidence dates from the late seventh and early eighth centuries, exhibiting deviations in wording, orthography, and the *suras*' order. An uneasy consensus posits that the received text evolved over perhaps a century, the "Uthmanic Codex" comprising the foundational (if not definitive) consonantal text. Meanwhile, vocalizations proliferated by the dozens until a tenth-century expert on the *hadith* declared seven traditions to have divine authority, a position that quickly gained accord. Today, the recitation of one of those seven, that of Asim ibn Abi al-Najud (d. 745), has gained worldwide ascendance as the reading used by the modern standard Quran produced in Egypt in 1924.

The Quran's most prominent message might be summarized as the imperative to believe in one God, God's messengers, books, and angels, and the Day of Judgment. It insists on God's absolute unity (*tawhid*): Allah is the transcendent "Lord of the Worlds" (Qur. 1:2), with whom one must never "associat[e] other gods" (Qur. 4:48). This abhorrence of polytheism and idolatry evolved into Muslims' fierce rejection of representing God and the prophets in human form—a sensibility resembling Jews' aversion to graven images, but foreign to Orthodox Christians' attraction to icons. The Quran demonstrates God's intimate involvement in human affairs not by narrating repeated providential interventions, as do the Deuteronomistic history and Acts, but by constantly invoking God's creation of the natural world and the manifest goodness within it: Allah brings rain that "revives" the dead earth, "signs [*ayat*] for people who understand" (Qur. 30:24). God's creation grounds the moral order. Like angels and *jinn*, humans are charged with obeying Allah, but they have both the obligation to steward the world and the capacity to tread the Straight Path (Qur. 1:6). They may sin—especially if they heed Satan's incessant whispers—but they can also repent.

To guide their decisions, God has sent generations of prophets, most notably Abraham, Moses, Jesus, and Muhammad, the final revelator and "seal" (Qur. 33:40). Though called "Messiah" (*al-Masih*), Jesus is not God's son but only a messenger—albeit a uniquely righteous one—who precedes Muhammad. Ethical concerns—such as caring for the poor or conducting business honestly—surface particularly in the Medinan passages concerned with the *umma*. Many verses reference the Last Judgment, at which time the dead shall be resurrected, although the Quran does not speculate as to when that event might occur. Believers will enjoy "extended shade, And overflowing water" (Qur. 56: 31–32), while unbelievers endure "Fire" relieved only by "water like molten brass" (Qur. 18:29). The Quran etches heaven and hell more vividly than either Tanakh or the New Testament ever attempt.

Through its self-presentation and subsequent Muslim reflection, the Quran has achieved a higher status in Islam than either Tanakh in Judaism or the Bible in Christianity. It calls itself "noble" and "hidden," Allah's "Revelation" that only "the purified" may touch (Qur. 56.77–80). These statements gird the widely held tenet that it is "uncreated"—that it existed eternally with God before being disclosed in historical time—and they guide its treatment. Much like the Torah (but unlike the Bible), the Quran is a sacrosanct object. Muslims deem it inimitable and therefore miraculous; when opponents scoffed that Muhammad must have "forged it," Allah directed his riposte: "Say, 'Come up then with ten forged surahs like it'" (Qur. 11:13). No one could. Its holiness inheres in its language, for Allah "revealed it as an Arabic Quran" (Qur. 12:2), a statement meant to express the text's accessibility and comprehensibility.

The Quran in Arabic is literally God's speech, hence any translation is necessarily imperfect and liturgically invalid. This exalted status grounds its view of the Jewish and Christian scriptures, simultaneously affirming and de-authorizing them. Revealed by prior prophets, those texts avow the truth, hence Jews and Christians are "People of the Book" (*Ahl al-Kitab*), but they have since corrupted their texts. Such contentions have also set the Quran as the keystone of Islamic culture. Millions of Muslims memorize it and declaim it daily, thereby reliving its original, oral transmission. It serves as the first source for Islamic law, the foundation for Arabic grammar, an inspiration for calligraphy, art, and architecture, and a touchstone for popular culture. Finally, it centers Islamic religious identity; however much Muslims may wrangle about law, doctrine, or practice, they all agree on what constitutes their sacred text.

Struggles over the caliphate (632–1258)

Forced to govern as well as preach, Muhammad in Medina was a prophet with exceptional civil power, given that the *umma* was a polity as well as a congregation. His death posed questions both about who should take charge and how this leader should exercise the position's conjoined responsibilities. Answers to the second question emerged over the next several centuries; the immediate issue concerned who would assume command, for Muhammad left no male heirs. Islamic history turned on how that choice was made—or is said to have been made. By some accounts, the Prophet named no successor, whereupon Umar ibn al-Khattab, a Companion, called a meeting of Helpers and Emigrants to acclaim Abu Bakr, another Companion, as caliph (*khalifa*, "successor" or "deputy"). Contemporaries seem to have accepted this decision, as did most Muslims subsequently. A minority, however, endorsed a different version: Muhammad had explicitly designated his cousin and son-in-law, Ali. They called themselves the Party of Ali (*Shiat Ali*)—precursor to the Shiite sect. The sources' vagaries render definitive historical assessment of all claims impossible. Although one scholar has made a plausible case that Muhammad did mean to choose Ali, inconsistencies in the evidence suggest that he left no clear plans. The three following caliphs—Umar, Uthman, and Ali—were similarly selected from among the Companions because of their family ties to the Prophet. Beginning in the ninth century, most Muslims would regard these four as "Rightly Guided Caliphs," and the Sunni sect would later avow that the *umma* had consented to them all.

The caliph was no prophet, but he was originally supposed, like Muhammad, to be the community's imam, an exemplar of righteousness. In the context of the *umma's* religious and political identity, this designation presumed that he both unified the *umma* through members' personal allegiance and guided them on God's course. The first caliphs probably decided legal cases and collated the Quran; they also took responsibility for defending the believers. After Abu Bakr subdued tribes that had renounced their political and religious allegiance to Muhammad following his death, Arab armies exploded out of their homeland. By 650 they had collapsed the Sasanid Empire, stripped Egypt and Palestine from the Byzantines, and were threatening Libya, eastern Iran, and Armenia. Their success owed much to the Sasanids and Byzantines having beaten each other down, along with the invaders' willingness to forego bloodshed if a target agreed to surrender and pay tribute. Recent research has qualified the assertion that non-Chalcedonian Christians facilitated Arab victories by welcoming the enemies of their Trinitarian persecutors: such expressions should be read as accommodation to new masters after the fact, rather than the desertion of old ones beforehand. Yet even as Umar and Uthman presided over a new empire's genesis, the premise that the caliph guided the *umma* occasioned discord. Rebels dissatisfied with Uthman assassinated him and proclaimed Ali as caliph, precipitating a civil war, with each side denouncing the other's leader as a false imam. An attempt to settle the conflict by arbitration angered some of Ali's erstwhile supporters, the Kharijites ("Seceders"), who concluded that he, too, was unfit to rule and killed him in 661. These events exposed the consequences of conceiving of the caliph as an imam. To practice the Prophet's religion, one had to align oneself with the proper guide. Disagreements over what the caliph's duties and character should be forced sectarian divisions within the *umma*.

Over the next few centuries, the nature of the caliphate changed, as what had been a loose polity in which Muslim Arabs ruled non-Muslims became a multiethnic Islamic empire. Following Ali's death, Muawiya, a member of Uthman's clan, founded the Umayyad dynasty (r. 661–750), basing the caliphate on the principle of hereditary succession. While extending their territory from Iberia to the Punjab, the Umayyads centralized the imperial machinery, moving the capital to Damascus and designating Arabic as the official administrative language. To legitimate their power, they molded an imperial ideology around an Islamic identity, proclaiming that the caliph is God's deputy, who exercises ultimate power to dispense divine law and deserves unquestioned obedience. The Dome of the Rock literally sets this idea in stone, trumpeting Islam's temporal and theological superiority over Judaism and Christianity. A shrine built in Byzantine style on the Temple site—where, according to Jews, Abraham had meant to sacrifice Isaac and, according to Muslims, Muhammad had ascended to heaven—the structure claims Abraham for Islam.

Nevertheless, the Umayyads seldom ruled unopposed. By the mid-eighth century, they faced widespread complaints about their perceived failure to guide the *umma* rightly. The *ulama*— independent scholars who had gained local reputations for their knowledge of religious law and counsel about proper practice— argued that they, not the caliph, possessed supreme religious authority. Others disputed the Umayyads' legitimacy as well: Kharijites insisted that the caliph be chosen on the basis of his dedication to "Quranic principles," not genealogy, while Ali's party held that the caliphate rightfully belonged to one of his direct heirs (Alids). In 750 a coalition driven by both pious revulsion against Umayyad pretensions and enthusiasm for Alid interests captured Damascus and installed Abu al-Abbas, who descended from an uncle of Muhammad.

The Abbasids (r. 750–1258) hoped to strengthen the empire and the prerogatives bequeathed by their predecessors. They built a new capital (Baghdad), rationalized the imperial bureaucracy, reorganized the army, encouraged intercontinental commerce, and promoted cultural activity. They strove to justify their rule in Islamic terms by both enacting policies, such as building mosques and appointing religious judges (*qadi*s), and advancing ideological claims, such as asserting their legitimacy by descent through the

Prophet's (extended) family and giving themselves titles designed to evoke unconditional obedience. Nevertheless, during their regime, the ideal of the caliph as the highest religious and political leader came apart for nearly all Muslims. The caliph Al-Mamun (r. 813–833) forced the *ulama* to accept the doctrine that the Quran is a created entity, but his inquisition backfired when the scholars successfully asserted that their superior ability to interpret the Quran and the traditions of the Prophet's exemplary behavior (*Sunna*) raised their religious stature above the caliph's. By the eleventh century, a Sunni identity had coalesced around a conception of the *umma* as an association (*Ahl al-Sunna wal Jamaa*, "People of the Tradition and the Community") that located religious authority in its consensual understanding of the Quran and the *Sunna* as interpreted by the *ulama*, regardless of who governed. Nor did the Abbasids' political headship remain intact. Their pretensions suffered insults from local secessionist movements, their relegation to serving as figureheads under Persian Shiite rule, and competition from caliphates declared in Iberia and Egypt. Their dispossession culminated when the Mongols captured Baghdad in 1258. Designed to unify the *umma*, the caliphate more frequently divided it.

Shiism (632–ca. 1000)

Early Christians fought over the nature of God and Christ. Early Muslims fought over who should lead the *umma*. This issue underlay the sectarian split between Sunnis and Shiites, identities that took several centuries to cohere, although both traditions projected their existence back into the seventh century. What became Shiism emerged among those who believed that, shortly before his death, Muhammad had explicitly conferred divinely sanctioned guardianship of the *umma* on Ali. Shiites built upon two memories electric with resentment against the majority's betrayal of Ali and the Prophet's family: the *umma*'s choice of Abu Bakr as first caliph; and the brutal defeat that the Umayyad caliph Yazid I inflicted on Husayn—Ali's younger son with the Prophet's daughter Fatima—at Karbala in 680, thereby securing Umayyad rule at the cost of martyring one of Muhammad's grandsons. In succeeding decades, "proto-Shiism" became more ethnically and theologically diverse, attracting non-Arabs and sifting through ideas—some quite esoteric—from Jewish, Christian, Zoroastrian, and other sources. Shiites eventually accepted a few of them—such as occultation (God's prolonged concealment of a living person from human contact). Special attention focused on propositions that the *umma* should be led by a divinely inspired Imam descended through the *Ahl al-Bayt* ("People of the [Prophet's] House")—a phrase that originally extended beyond the Alids. Still, many who supported the Abbasid revolt expected that the victors would appoint an Alid, only to suffer the Abbasids' assertion that their line—a branch collateral to the Prophet's—lay closer to the Prophet than did Ali's.

Shiism took shape as a recognizable religious movement from the eighth to tenth centuries in anxious relationship with both the Abbasids, ever alert for Alid rebelliousness, and the majority of Muslims, who generally accepted the legitimacy of the caliphs prior to Ali and resisted vesting supreme religious influence in a single person. During and after the Abbasid revolution, religious scholars began to crystallize a cohesive theological identity. The most prominent was Jafar al-Sadiq, who became a fountainhead of Shiite (and Sunni) jurisprudence as well as (for most Shiites) the sixth Imam. He determined that the imamate ran through Hasan (Fatima's older son), Husayn, and thence through Husayn's direct male descendants, a calculus most Shiites accepted. For their part, the Abbasids tended to keep the Shiites close, prompting Jafar and others to elaborate the principle of *taqiyya*: someone under severe threat may dissemble about one's religious beliefs without sin. For those who counted Jafar as the sixth Imam, a crisis opened in 874 when the eleventh Imam died, apparently without heir. One of his agents disclosed the existence of a young son who had been concealed to escape persecution. The child never appeared to his followers personally, but he was said to contact them via emissaries, the last of whom died in 941. Theologians worked out the implications. The twelfth—and final—Imam, they said, had gone into occultation, during which time he will remain inaccessible except through miraculous intervention. As *al-Mahdi* (the "Righteous One"), he will rule the earth justly before the Last Judgment. So-called "Twelver" Shiites (Ithnaasharis) await the "Hidden Imam's" return.

Shiites differentiated themselves from Sunnis doctrinally by rejecting the caliphate and anchoring headship of the *umma* entirely in an Imam, a lineal descendant of Ali. The imamate reconstituted ultimate religious (and, depending on the sect, political) power in a single person entrusted with sole authority to guide the *umma* along the proper Islamic path. Given this charge, the Imam had to be an exemplary individual graced with unsurpassed religious knowledge, as well as the capacity to interpret revelation infallibly. Unlike the caliphate, whose transmission depends on communal consensus, the imamate passes from incumbent to successor through divinely inspired designation. Endowed with Muhammad's power of interpreting revelation (although not with his prophetic calling to establish it), the Imam is a sign (*aya*) of Allah's constant kindness toward human beings. Shiites also marked themselves devotionally by making pilgrimages to shrines of their Imams. Such processions mingled expressions of love for the Prophet's family with dismay over its treatment: the angels, runs one ancient elegy, wept "copiously" upon viewing Umayyad lances at Karbala bearing Husayn's and his followers' heads. Against Sunnis' status as the Muslim "mainstream" (roughly 85 percent at present), much Shii self-perception throbs with minority grievance and grief, a lamentation that they have taken the right course while history and the majority have not.

No single understanding of the imamate united the Shia. A rebellion against the Umayyads fomented by Zayd bin Ali, a grandson of Husayn, occasioned a particularly political version.

Although the uprising failed, it provided a model figure who leads the *umma* by resisting tyranny. Zaydi Imams are legitimized by their abilities to mobilize supporters and mount an armed uprising, qualifications that deemphasize the Imam's religious role: his legal rulings hold no special weight, and Zaydis may at times choose no Imam. The succession crisis following Jafar al-Sadiq's death generated another sect, for his presumed heir, Ismail, had predeceased him. The eventual Twelvers theorized that God's decree had changed, and they settled on another son, but a different faction claimed Ismail as their seventh Imam. Ismailis agree with Twelvers about strict succession, inerrancy, and the necessity of always having an Imam, but they grant each Imam such autonomy that he may entirely redefine his community's theology and law. At times, Ismailis took a far more robust position on the Imam's political qualifications. In the nineteenth and twentieth centuries, however, the Nizaris—currently the largest Ismaili group—resurfaced in south Asia and then parts of Europe with an Imam (known as the Aga Khan) who approximates being the absolute head of an international nongovernmental organization. In contrast, the Twelvers essentially eliminated the Imam's political presence once the Twelfth Imam went into occultation.

Islam's rapid ascension to governing power, coupled with the ideal that only a manifestly pious ruler could lead the *umma* to God, helps explain why political quarrels among Muslims precipitated sectarian schisms. It may also illumine the distinctive mix of ethnic particularism (that is, the prominence accorded the Arab heritage) and theological universalism (namely, the proclamation that Allah is "your Lord and my Lord" [Qur. 19:36]) that came to color Islam's identity. Although preaching the One God whose sanctuary is a house "for all peoples" (Isa. 56:7), Judaism was the tradition of *Am Yisrael*, a people whom both they and their neighbors stamped as different religiously and culturally. Christianity proclaimed the Gospel "to all nations" (Luke 24:47) and divested itself of any "Jewish" ethnic identity a few centuries before it won the Roman throne. Islam, meanwhile, constructed itself in between those stances. It likely began as an Arab monotheism, but empire catalyzed its contact with non-Arabs, who in due course converted, integrated themselves into Islamic polities, and eventually ruled them. As a result, Islam neither totally detached itself from its founders' ethnicity (as did Christianity) nor elevated its identity and language to exclusive status (as did Judaism). Instead, it ended up a hybrid, privileging its ethnic origins even as non-Arab Muslims began to outnumber Arab ones. It was empire, too, that structured Muslims' increasing—and increasingly complex—interactions with Jews and Christians.

Chapter 5
Medieval interactions (700–1500)

Islam's close association with the state influenced the development of its theology and law; the latter became the leading discipline for ordering Islamic societies and for framing Muslims' interactions with Christians and Jews. The association of both Christianity and Islam with state power encouraged ideologies that could justify military action against the other, most notably the Crusades. Religious minorities—Jews and Christians in Muslim lands; Jews and Muslims in Christian territory—often lived restricted lives, yet Christian and especially Muslim practice sometimes allowed for toleration as well as extensive cultural and intellectual exchange, albeit without ceding political control.

Islamic theology

Theology's place within Islam owed much to historical circumstance. Unlike Christianity, which had to painstakingly distinguish itself from Judaism, Islam separated from its Abrahamic predecessors without much doctrinal fuss. The Quran's claims that Jews and Christians had received truth but corrupted God's word opened space for a new revelation. Compared to Christian divinity, Islamic theology operated less in response to abstract speculation than to politics. The first controversies arose during the seventh-century fights over choosing the caliph. Ali's party alleged that, because of Uthman's and Muawiya's sins, they and their followers had forfeited their place in the *umma*—charges the Umayyads reciprocated. Kharijites maintained that only uncompromising obedience to the law upheld one's membership; professions of faith did not matter. A more generous assessment of a believer's community standing— which became the standard—emerged among Muslims distressed at partisan fractures. Murjites ("Deferrers") asserted that only God could judge a person's faith, and they accepted all but the most heinous sinners. These arguments raised questions about whether God predetermines human actions or allows free will. Kharijites implied that individuals are independent moral actors, a stance criticized as undercutting God's omnipotence. Determinism bolstered Umayyads' claims to rule by de-emphasizing personal responsibility for error and crediting the clan's ascendance to Allah's will, not human initiative (although not all who upheld determinism supported the dynasty).

Theological speculation became more systematic as Muslims expanded their intellectual reach, a consequence of the early Abbasid program to integrate the empire's different cultures under Islam. Seeking to acquire practical knowledge in the arts and sciences, the state sponsored the *Bayt al-Hikma* ("House of Wisdom") in Baghdad, where scholars—including non-Muslims— translated Syriac, Persian, Hindu, and Greek texts into Arabic. Doctors of *kalam* (usually translated as "theology") wielded philosophical arguments to quell believers' doubts and defend Islam. Among the first practitioners were the Mutazilites, theologians who favored methods of rational analysis to devise doctrine. They denied that the Quran is coeternal with God, a thesis they thought inconsistent with *tawhid*, the concept of God's absolute unity. Caliph Al-Mamun's project to force conformity to this principle inspired resistance from such traditionalists as Ahmad ibn Hanbal, who insisted that the Quran is indeed coeternal and preferred to accept the certainty of such propositions "without asking how," as he put it, rather than by using reason. A former Mutazilite, Abu al-Hasan al-Ashari, steered between the extreme rationalist and traditionalist positions. Deploying Mutazilite methods to refute their conclusions, he declared that God's power to ordain human acts is nevertheless consistent with individuals having free will and thus moral responsibility for their deeds. Accepting al-Ashari's synthesis, Sunnis rejected Mutazilite rationalism, but Twelver and Zaidi Shiites embraced it. Unlike theology's eminence in Christianity, *kalam* has generally occupied a lesser place among the Islamic religious sciences—those subjects, such as law, ethics, metaphysics, and even economics, that teach Muslims how to live as God wishes.

Islamic philosophy (*falsafa*) assumed a similar status. It germinated in the environment that nurtured *kalam* and harbored a similarly apologetic goal, but it differed by not basing itself on the Quran and by asserting its supreme ability to conceive of God truthfully. *Falsafa* drew heavily on Greek thinking, and its advocates addressed matters from ontology to politics. Ibn Sina—philosopher, astronomer, and physician—devised the first holistic system: the universe is a rational structure in which God is the initial cause of events but cannot change the laws of nature. While refuting criticisms to *falsafa* and refining its method, Ibn Rushd—another wide-ranging thinker—proposed that both religion and philosophy can make true statements, although the latter's are the most perfect. But *falsafa* faced intense opposition, most bitingly from Abu Hamid al-Ghazali, who denounced its "fanciful notions" as internally inconsistent and utterly faithless. Such jibes stuck, and by the fourteenth century, *kalam* had essentially absorbed *falsafa* almost everywhere. Particularly among Sunnis, tradition's authority bested that of reason. Ibn Sina (Avicenna, as he was called in the Christian West) and Ibn Rushd (known there as Averroes) had greater impact on Christian and Jewish philosophers than on Muslim ones.

Islamic law

There is much merit in the truism that Christianity esteems "correct thought" (orthodoxy) while Islam (and Judaism) value "right behavior" (orthopraxy). Of Islam's "five pillars"—testimony ("there is no god but God" and Muhammad is his "Messenger"), prayer, alms, fasting, and pilgrimage—only the first concerns right belief. Unsurprisingly, adjudicating how a good Muslim should live became the preeminent religious concern. Like rabbinic law, Islamic law took the form of an open-ended discourse about how to analyze core texts, rather than how to apply a statutory code. Identifying those texts and devising proper interpretations required several centuries. Decisions rendered under the Umayyads by local judges drew haphazardly upon the Quran and other materials and were mediated by neighborhood custom or speculation.

As an increasingly multicultural Muslim population lost confidence that rulings so obtained accurately represented the traditions of Muhammad and his Companions, groups of legal experts—most notably Muhammad b. Idris al-Shafii and his students—transferred religious authority from the *umma*'s lived practice to what became a canonical set of sacred written materials. Al-Shafii identified the *hadith* as a second textual repository of divine revelation alongside the Quran. Over the next few generations, his followers transformed the sites of legal discussion from diffuse groups touting their particular leader's legal advice into schools of law (*maddhab*s) that advanced systematized principles and techniques. By creating a science of interpretation embedded in a scholarly community, al-Shafii and his followers penned the blueprints that framed Islamic law and made it central to the construction of Muslim identity.

That science—jurisprudence (*fiqh*, "understanding")—builds on four fundamentals: two substantive, two methodological. The Quran outlines legal and moral principles but provides few specifics, hence the *Sunna*'s status as a second site of inspiration. During the ninth and tenth centuries, its "canonization" precipitated a massive effort to authenticate *hadith* that winnowed perhaps as many as a million items into the 5,000 found among the six collections that Sunnis deem the most theologically sound. Some researchers question the *hadiths*' reliability, flagging anachronisms and charging that jurists invented or forged them. Others retort that at least some demonstrably date to the seventh century and that the effort taken to verify them—an exercise unparalleled in other premodern cultures—warrants confidence in their genuineness. Dismissing all *hadith* as untrustworthy is surely too extreme. For Muslims, in any case, the argument is moot.

Fiqh is formulated as legal scholars apply independent reasoning (*ijtihad*) to the Quran and *Sunna*. *Ijtihad*'s fundamental tool is analogical reasoning: judgment that a novel case can, in the absence of existing law, be settled by deducing its similarity to a previous case and transposing the operative legal principle from the old case to the new. A ruling becomes *fiqh* when jurists endorse it by consensus. The standardization of sources and procedures notwithstanding, *fiqh* in practice is hardly uniform. From what were once dozens of local schools, four came to predominate among Sunnis, each deriving its theories, practice, and name from its founder: Abu Hanifa, Malik ibn Anas, al-Shafii, or ibn Hanbal. While they disagree over interpretations and legal substance, these bodies concluded by the tenth century that they shared major premises and that the most important issues had been settled. This accord underwrote their assent to each other's legitimacy (thereby acknowledging a de facto "legal pluralism") and the postulate that future jurists should exercise *taqlid* ("imitation"), tethering their decision-making to each *madhhab*'s tradition. *Taqlid* was meant to stabilize legal rulings and protect the *ulama*'s religious authority against a ruler's encroachments; whether it also may have curbed independent reasoning and hampered *fiqh*'s ability to address changing social conditions is a matter historians and Islamic legal scholars debate.

Shia approach legal sources and methods somewhat differently. Most consider the Imam an infallible source, along with the Quran and *Sunna*. They reference four major collections of *hadith*, whose lines of transmission run through their Imams and reflect some characteristic interests, such as emphasizing reports about Muhammad's family. Methodologically, they defer to the Imam, rejecting analogy and consensus. Sources of *fiqh* diverge among sects. Twelvers follow Jafar al-Sadiq's *madhhab*; in the Hidden Imam's absence, interpretive authority falls to highly esteemed scholars. In contrast, Ismailis and Zaydis have tended to vest that authority in their Imams, rather than in jurists.

Understood in the most liberal sense, Islamic law is the structure that guides a Muslim's life according to God's will. The term that conveys this sense is *Sharia* ("path"), a divine call to Muslims about the ideal way to live. A framework simultaneously legal, religious, and moral, *Sharia* governs one's relationships with both God and other human beings. To translate "*Sharia*" simply as "Islamic law" (or "Islamic law" exclusively as "*Sharia*") can be misleading, since non-Muslims (and Muslims) have variously construed it as state-codified religious law, as a synonym for *fiqh*, or as any law aiming to promote justice and social welfare. In its usual formulation, *Sharia* is not positive law, but a godly epitome actualized in *fiqh* by legal experts conscious of their fallibility. *Sharia* is one, but *fiqh* is multiple. Moreover, *Sharia* includes more than *fiqh*.

Sharia developed in close proximity to the state, but in a manner that balanced power between the sovereign and religious scholars. The Abbasids' effort to impose an orthodox understanding of the Quran instead resulted in an empowered *ulama* and, among Sunnis, signaled law's dominance over theology as a means of accommodating interpretive differences within a shared Islamic identity. In most Islamic polities before European colonizers disrupted customary arrangements, *fiqh* developed independently of state control. *Qadi*s appointed by the sovereign settled cases in religious courts, but they applied rules generated by author-jurists and glossed by *mufti*s (private legal consultants) who issued *fatwa*s, nonbinding but influential findings about points at issue. The sovereign enjoyed free rein over his own legal sphere, *siyasa* ("administration," "policy"), which dealt with such matters as regulating markets and keeping the peace. Arbitrated in its own courts, *siyasa* nonetheless fell under *Sharia* because its concern with the public interest coincided with *Sharia*'s basic principles. Conceived as subsets of *Sharia*, *fiqh* and *siyasa* were both presumed to be necessary to the maintenance of an Islamic society's just order. How they interacted depended on the influence of the *ulama* relative to that of the potentate, who might prefer one school's jurists or fund its schools. As a subset of *Sharia*, *siyasa* legitimized a state's Islamic identity, but the sovereign, not the *ulama*, determined *siyasa*'s content. Conversely, the state enforced *fiqh* but did not dictate its content. When applied outside Muslim communities, this logic allowed the possibility for designated minorities to enjoy religious (but not political) autonomy over their own affairs, an arrangement that took shape as Muslims, Christians, and Jews engaged each other in both war and peace.

The Crusades (1095–ca. 1400)

The defeat of Muslim armies at Constantinople (717–718) and Tours (732) blunted Islam's European ambitions and foreshadowed an ongoing struggle with Christians in and around the Mediterranean Sea. By 1050, a multitude of Christian domains faced a fragmented array of Muslim polities, including the disintegrating Abbasid caliphate, and an Egyptian imamate—the Ismaili (Shiite) Fatimids—that was contesting the (Sunni) Seljuk Turks for Syria and Palestine. A standoff persisted until the late eleventh century, when the Seljuks drove the Byzantines from Asia

Minor, and Latin Europe launched an unprecedented incursion into the eastern Mediterranean precipitated by two mounting concerns. Access to the Holy Land was one. Christian pilgrimages, which the Arab conquests had never entirely stalled, accelerated during the eleventh century, but rumors that wayfarers risked robbery or death fueled desires to retake the lands Jesus had walked. The reversal of Byzantine fortunes was a second concern, leading Emperor Alexius I Comnenus to solicit the papacy for mercenaries to help stave off the Seljuks. Had he known what was coming, he might have reconsidered. In 1095, Pope Urban II urged Christians to storm the Holy Land, alleging habitual torture of pilgrims. Appealing to a Christian unity more aspirational than actual, he may have wanted to heal the breach with Eastern Orthodoxy and assert papal supremacy as well as to liberate Jerusalem. Whatever his motives, the call launched an era of crusades.

Powerful ideologies justifying religious violence motivated combatants on both sides. For centuries, Christians had manifested a profound ambivalence toward war. The Gospels are filled with images of Jesus as a peacemaker: if struck on the right cheek, he taught, "turn the other also" (Matt. 5:39). For a millennium, the clergy required soldiers who killed in combat to do penance for their sin. Still, the Bible inherited Tanakh's imagery of YHWH as captain of the Chosen People, and the book of Revelation revels in the slaughter to be inflicted on the faithless and the Church's enemies, both human and cosmic, at the Apocalypse. Once the Roman Empire embraced Christianity, the Church could comfortably justify war in the state's defense. Augustine laid down a general theory of a just war: it is undertaken in defense and to right a wrong. This essentially legal definition could also accommodate a more passionate rationale: a holy war willed by God is also just. By the late eleventh century, conditions in Western Christendom had become ripe for taking holy war theory a step further. In promising a plenary indulgence—remission of sin and satisfaction for penance—to all who bore arms to the Holy Land, Urban II condoned war in God's name as itself a penitential act, thereby sanctioning forgiveness for carnage.

Though it too cited God's approval for bloodshed, the concept of *jihad* emerged from a different historical setting—the *umma*'s earliest efforts to define and defend itself—and intellectual locus. A preeminently legal rather than theological category, *jihad* in a religious context means "striving [for God's sake]" and constitutes a perpetual obligation. Jurists distinguished between what they called the "greater" *jihad*—personal spiritual labor to surmount one's imperfections—and the "lesser" *jihad*—physical combat to expand and protect Islam, usually considered a collective responsibility (although incumbent on individuals under certain conditions). The lesser *jihad* presumed that Islam ought to embrace the entire world, which divided into *Dar al-Islam* (the "Abode of Islam," lands under Islamic law) and *Dar al-Harb* (the "Abode of War," the realm of non-Muslim polities). *Dar al-Harb* was open to attack—if conditions allowed, and then only in accordance with rules of engagement that required legitimate authorization and the proper conduct toward noncombatants.

Shiites wrote their own treatments, in which authority to summon *jihad* rested with the Imam (or, for Twelvers, his designates). In practice, conducting *jihad* reflected historical circumstances. The most bellicose constructions appeared at the height of Islamic imperial expansion, but, as borders stabilized, Muslim sovereigns sometimes invoked *jihad* more to legitimize themselves than to gain territory, while jurists designed legal mechanisms to facilitate peaceful contacts. In places far from contested frontiers, the call for belligerent *jihad* went dormant. When the first European forces arrived, styling themselves "soldiers of Christ" gave them an initial motivational advantage over their adversaries.

The Crusades may be defined as papally authorized campaigns in which volunteers vowed to fight for Christianity in return for spiritual rewards. The original targets were Muslims, and the initial operation (1095–1099, enumerated the "First Crusade" only later) achieved the most spectacular success, primarily because it capitalized (unwittingly) on a period of maximum disorganization and infighting within and among Muslim states. Armies recruited from western and central Europe (called "Franks" in recognition of the large numbers who came from France) captured Jerusalem in July 1099, exulting in the "blood of the slain" (which, according to a Muslim account, included Jews burned in their synagogue). Although historians now reject estimates numbering the dead in the tens of thousands as exaggerations, the massacre and its aftershocks—the Dome of the Rock turned into an abbey church; four Crusader states stretched along and beyond the Levantine coast—slowly catalyzed a Muslim countercrusade. The formula for successfully prosecuting it came from the *ulama*, who sought to galvanize Muslims by linking the greater and lesser *jihad*s.

Having diagnosed defeat as the consequence of moral failure, scholars prescribed raising fighters whose own spiritual struggles would commit them to the defense of Islam, captained by warrior-leaders whose personal virtues could unify the *umma*. Edessa's capture in 1144 by the Zengid Turks demonstrated what a reimagined *jihad* might achieve. The city's fall triggered the Second Crusade (1145–1149), which, from a Frankish perspective, failed dismally. Salah al-Din (Saladin) personified the warrior-sultan ideal, consolidating a new Sunni state under his Ayyubite dynasty and retaking Jerusalem in 1187. France, England, and the Holy Roman Empire quickly launched the Third Crusade (1188–1192), during which England's King Richard I secured pilgrims' continuing access to Jerusalem, though not its possession. Subsequent crusades to the Holy Land accomplished little, and the last Latin state fell in 1291.

But crusading did not stop, nor were Muslims the Christians' only foes. The impulse to launch holy wars discovered additional targets in and around Christendom. Plotted as an attempt to establish a strategic beachhead in Egypt, the Fourth Crusade (1198–1204) never confronted a Muslim; it concluded with soldiers sacking Constantinople and founding a Latin empire that lasted until 1261, permanently alienating the Greek Church from Rome. Popes sometimes invoked crusades against political rivals or competing claimants to Peter's throne. Other crusades recalled ancient concerns about suppressing heterodoxy. The presence in southern France of Cathars—who sought spiritual purity by renouncing the material world—inspired the Albigensian Crusade (1209–1229), which featured mass executions and degenerated into a land grab by the French aristocracy. The Church never directed crusades at Jews specifically, but preaching against Christ's enemies aggravated resentment over their visibility as moneylenders, instigating collective violence in the Rhineland and England. Drives for Jerusalem ended in the thirteenth century, but holy wars against the Ottoman Empire and alleged heretics continued into the sixteenth.

The Crusades loom large in popular imaginings of the Middle Ages, but their impacts on both Western Christendom and *Dar al-Islam* were mixed. Within Latin Christianity they elevated the importance of indulgences as a means to remit punishment owed for one's sins and fed existing inclinations to persecute the Church's enemies. Politically, they had greater bearing, ironically, on areas remote from the Middle Eastern theater of operations, where the Latin states disappeared after two centuries, and where the occupation of Byzantium may have been less instrumental in the Byzantine Empire's ongoing decline than some have surmised. Nearer to home, they reintegrated Iberia and brought parts of the Baltic into Latin Christendom.

Within Islam, a major religious ramification of the Crusades was the elaboration of *jihad* doctrine—which Sunnis aimed also at Shiites. Jerusalem grew more prominent as an object of Muslims' pious desire. The Crusades' greatest legacy may have been cultural, in the long run. In the shorter run, Muslims celebrated

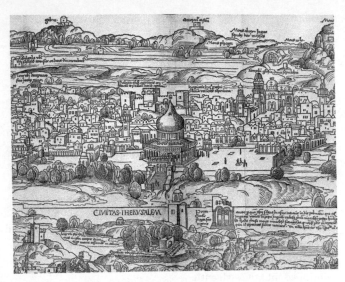

CIVITAS IHERVSALEM

**6. The Temple Mount (called by Muslims "the Noble Sanctuary")
takes center stage in a view of late fifteenth-century Jerusalem that
accompanied a contemporary pilgrim's account. Perceiving the site in
Christian terms, the woodcut virtually disregards most of the Muslim
buildings in the city and calls the outsized Dome of the Rock
"Solomon's Temple," an identification going back to the Crusades.**

their victories but did not conceive events as having amounted to
a distinctively Christian invasion until the nineteenth century,
when contemporary European imperial ventures triggered
disquieting memories of having lost power and status long ago.
Since then, distrust of Europe and the United States as ravening
"Crusaders" has only intensified, particularly among radical
Islamists, who allege parallels between the Latin states and
modern Israel, seeing both as fortified intrusions onto Muslim
ground propped up with Christian arms and money.

Religious minorities in Christendom and *Dar al-Islam* (ca. 700–ca. 1500)

The Crusades represented only one variety of interreligious experience. Christians and Muslims routinely inhabited each other's jurisdictions, as did Jews, who normally did not run their own state. *Dar al-Islam* and Christendom constructed the rules governing treatment of their religious minorities according to very different principles. Muslims acknowledged Jews, Christians, and (eventually) others as "People of the Book" who worshiped God (however imperfectly) and so, unlike pagans, they were not subject to religious "compulsion" (Qur. 2:256). This determination grounded a special legal category, *ahl al-dhimma* ("protected people"). "Dhimmitude" ordinarily promised Jews and Christians security and internal autonomy over their religious communities while imposing obligations, such as an annual poll tax (*jizya*), and denying them the right to rebuild their houses of worship or convert Muslims.

*Dhimmi*s occupied a recognized if inferior place under Muslim rule. Christian sovereigns, in contrast, developed no such universal framework; statutes governing religious minorities in any particular polity might derive from Roman or Byzantine precedents, but they also reflected local concerns and lacked any binding theological imperative. Christians might tolerate Jews because Jews' existence "proved" Christianity's superiority, and they might engage Muslims to benefit themselves even though Muslims followed an "untrue" religion. Together, pragmatism and prejudice could result in Christians treating Jews and Muslims like *dhimmi*s, but any arrangements depended ultimately on the ruler's whims, and minorities' legal position was more fragile in Christendom than in Muslim lands. Expulsions and forced conversions happened more readily under Christian than Muslim regimes. In both locales, toleration meant subordination, never equality. The ways in which Muslims and Christians regarded religious subgroups was always conditional and ranged from accepting to murderous.

Most Jews lived in Muslim-held Palestine, Iraq (Babylonia), and Egypt. Largely spared persecution, they built international trading networks, which helped foster a sense of solidarity among far-flung Jewish communities. Muslims' largesse did not reflect any particular affection for Jews, however. Muslims harbored an elemental ambivalence about them that dated to their rejection of Muhammad as a prophet: the Jewish proclamation of One God was true, but the Jews who professed it had almost always proved false. Yet that attitude embedded political enmities more strongly than theological ones and could be blunted by perceptions of Islam's success, Jews' political invisibility, and both parties' vigorous dismissal of the Trinity.

Conditions within *Dar al-Islam*—permeable borders, expanding trade networks, and a common language (Arabic)—helped spread a relatively standardized version of rabbinic Judaism more extensively than ever before. Jews shared the heady intellectual atmosphere of early Abbasid Baghdad, where Rabbi Saadia Gaon applied Mutazilite *kalam* to square Jewish tradition with Greek philosophy—in Arabic. Wider synchronicities may be discerned in the work of the Masoretes, Jewish scholars who, likely following in the footsteps of Muslim counterparts stabilizing the Quran's text, had by the end of the tenth century standardized the Tanakh's text, vowels, and punctuation. As the Abbasid caliphate declined, Jews such as Maimonides migrated to Egypt. An ethicist, Mishnaic scholar, and conversation partner with Muslim intellectuals, Maimonides also served Saladin as court physician. His life exemplifies the vicissitudes *dhimmi*s might experience. Driven into a public "conversion" to Islam by the Moroccan Almohads—Berbers who demanded that all *dhimmi*s accept Islam and that all Muslims acquiesce to the Almohads' rigorous unitarianism—he advocated dissembling about one's true religious beliefs under threat (a doctrine similar to *taqiyya*). In Egypt he practiced Judaism openly, and a Muslim jurist invalidated his conversion as contrary to *Sharia*. Ayyubid liberality did not survive into the Mamluk dynasty (1250–1517), which—perhaps sensing a contraction of *Dar al-Islam*'s political and economic vitality—enforced the *dhimmi* laws more harshly.

During the early Middle Ages, new Jewish communities mushroomed in the Rhineland, Provence, and England, as rulers sought migrants to stimulate commercial development. Compared with their co-religionists in *Dar al-Islam*, Jews in Christian Europe were more occupationally confined, culturally isolated, and socially exposed. Civil and ecclesiastical laws often protected their property and religious practice, but implementation depended on rulers who claimed Jews as a unique class of dependents and juggled competing incentives: protect them to maintain public order and collect their taxes; or flog them, especially if the Church tagged them as deviants or popular resentment against them (and their patrons) flared. Yet, into the eleventh century, Jews often enjoyed prosperity and neighborly relations. The Rhineland massacre during the First Crusade signaled a long deterioration in their status as the Church hardened its stance against heterodoxy and the populace chafed at Jews' perceived economic privileges. Anti-Jewish polemic shifted from depicting them as theological figments to branding them as satanic menaces who ritually murdered Christians, desecrated the Host, and poisoned wells. Exterminations, both individual and communal, often followed such accusations, despite efforts by princes to avert and church leaders to rebut them. Intellectual exchange did occur—Jews adopted some Christian techniques of exegesis and formatting the biblical text, and a few Christian scholars studied Hebrew sources—but theological discourse usually involved disputations staged mainly to confirm Christian truth or convert Jews. Declining economic utility and intensifying vilification sped their expulsion from England, France, Germany, and Spain.

Most Christians within *Dar al-Islam* lived in Egypt, Syria, Palestine, and Iraq, having crystallized into autonomous churches. Compared to Jews—who were long accustomed to inhabiting other cultures and for whom Muslim rule opened opportunities such as Umar's invitation to resettle Jerusalem in 638—Christians likely experienced the Arab conquests more traumatically. Coming to terms with their new situation, they had within a couple of centuries made Arabic their vernacular and scriptural language. They held positions as civil administrators and physicians and had prominent places in the Abbasid "House of Wisdom," where Hunayn ibn Ishaq, a Nestorian ("two-nature") Christian, translated the Septuagint as well as works of medicine, science, and philosophy. Officially forbidden to proselytize Muslims, churches nevertheless sent missionaries to Iran and beyond. Christians' fortunes (like Jews') fluctuated. Majority populations at the conquest, they gradually became minorities primarily through voluntary conversion, a choice they undertook more readily than Jews did. From the eleventh century on, Christians' position became more precarious, as the Seljuks' and Ayyubids' militant Sunnism, coupled with suspicions of native Christians heightened by the Crusades and Mongol invasions, led to periodic stiffening of restrictions, mob violence, and even the transformation of churches into mosques. Amid everything, believers constructed an "Arab Christianity" simultaneously splintered by denominational identities and unified by the well-calculated habit of using Islamic idioms to voice Christian claims about the Trinity and the Incarnation—such as calling Jesus (like Allah) "Lord of the Worlds."

Medieval Iberia, especially *al-Andalus* (the Muslim-ruled portion) has drawn particular notice as the foremost locale in which Jews, Christians, and Muslims practiced *convivencia* ("living together"). Such an assessment warrants qualification. Over its nearly eight-century existence, *al-Andalus* was ruled by regimes with very different policies toward *dhimmi*s. As Christians relentlessly retook the peninsula (the *Reconquista*), minorities shuttled across shifting borders while spaces of peaceful coexistence opened—and shut. The notion of there having been a golden age does have plausibility. Tenth-century Córdoba boasted a Jewish court physician and libraries flush with Abbasid translations; its caliphs supported and employed Jews and Christians as bureaucrats and scholars. Prosperous, fluent in Arabic, and usually secure, Jewish elites in *al-Andalus* exhibited a cultural vibrancy, using Arabic forms and themes to transform Hebrew into a vehicle for writing vernacular poetry, for example, and sparring candidly with Muslim counterparts over religion and philosophy. Yet *convivencia* was always conditional; in 1066, Muslims assassinated Granada's Jewish vizier and ravaged the Jewish quarter. The conquest of Seville in 1147 by the Almohads precipitated Jews' flight to Christian sanctuaries, stimulating another multireligious project already underway. In Toledo, Jews and *mudéjares* (Muslims inhabiting Christian territory) translated

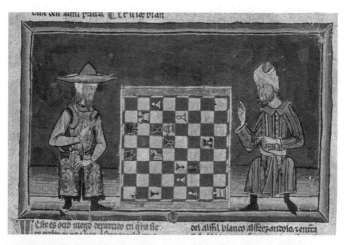

7. A Jew and a Muslim play chess in *El Libro de los Juegos* (*The Book of the Games*), completed in 1283. This book is an example of King Alfonso X's project to have Muslim and Jewish as well as Christian scholars translate works from Arabic and Hebrew into Castilian and Latin.

Arabic texts orally into Castilian speech, which Christians transcribed into Latin, completing Europe's reappropriation of its Greco-Roman heritage—by way of Baghdad.

Meanwhile, hardened attitudes toward Jews and continuing enmity against Moorish enemies altered the religious terrain. In 1252, King Alfonso X of Castile—though a patron of Jewish and Muslim scholars—nevertheless ordered Toledo's Jews and *mudéjares* to kneel when they encountered the Host in a public procession. Pogroms in 1391 killed perhaps a third of Spain's Jews and coerced another third to convert to Christianity. The loyalties of these *conversos* ("New Christians") and of *moriscos* (converts from Islam) proved a constant worry; the Inquisition, originally ecclesiastical courts charged with suppressing heretics, determined to roust crypto-Jews and -Muslims. With the *Reconquista*'s culmination in 1492, *limpieza de sangre* ("purity of blood")—the mark of a "true" Spanish Catholic—trumped *convivencia*; the Spanish monarchy thrust out unconverted Jews in that year and practicing Muslims in 1525.

Al-Andalus was neither heaven nor hell for *dhimmi*s, but rather a place in which they sometimes thrived and sometimes suffered. It thus exemplified how Judaism, Christianity, and Islam are not fixed entities, but traditions whose adherents have constantly engaged each other for both good and ill.

Chapter 6
Reform and Enlightenment (1500–1900)

Since 1500, Judaism, Christianity, and Islam have had to define themselves within spaces shaped by the global expansion of (Christian) European empires, growing skepticism of revealed religion, and the emergence of nation-states. These changes unsettled the familiar ways in which Jews, Christians, and Muslims understood their traditions, spurring movements of reform and renewal. The Reformation divided the Western Church, further complicating Christian identity. The Enlightenment elevated reason and empirical evidence over revelation and received wisdom as the preeminent paths to knowledge, challenging religion's stature. As European power and influence expanded, Muslims sought to preserve Islam's fundamentals. The Jewish Enlightenment, meanwhile, birthed a movement that challenged some of Judaism's long-standing foundations.

Reform in the Western churches, ca. 1500–ca. 1650

In 1500 one could still imagine Europe as a Christian domain in which the Pope headed the universal Church, upheld the faith, and kept moral watch in conjunction with temporal rulers who—like virtually everyone else in these lands, which were nearly void of Jews and Muslims—were "good Christians." But the reality was messier. The papacy endured a schism (1378–1417) during which dueling claimants established rival courts. In England, John Wyclif proclaimed the Bible's authority over the Pope's; in Bohemia, Jan Hus catalyzed the formation of a church that retained most Catholic rites but declared itself independent of Rome. Humanist scholars challenged the Latin Bible's text, questioning theological deductions and interpretive methods dependent on it. But no one anticipated rending the entire ecclesiastical structure, not—initially, at least—Martin Luther, the thirtysomething professor who in 1517 denounced the sale of papal indulgences as "nets" used by the Church to "fish" for wealth. How Luther helped inaugurate a transformation of the Western Church had much to do with his and other reformers' belief that the Church needed an overhaul, the efforts by the Pope and the Holy Roman Emperor to suppress them, the support they received from sympathetic princes (the first people to call themselves "Protestants"), and their ability to circulate new ideas quickly through the medium of print. The Eastern Church escaped such disruption, perhaps because it did not boast a universal head, missed (and dismissed) the import of Protestant critiques, or—having always read the New Testament in Greek—never built its credibility on a translation.

The Reformation was, first and foremost, a religious argument centered on the machinery of salvation and the Church's perceived (in)ability to work the levers. Three major issues divided Protestants from Catholics (and sometimes from themselves). The first involved explaining how God justifies sinners—that is, makes or accounts them as righteous. Luther had rendered Romans 1:17 as affirming that the righteous live "by faith alone." Protestants held that God bestows grace freely, not in response to human initiative, and declares sinners just by imputing Christ's merit to them. In contrast, Catholics underlined the human response to divine grace and maintained that God imparts Christ's merit to assenting individuals. A second disagreement concerned how to determine the ultimate source for proper doctrine and practice. Protestants insisted on scripture's singular authority; Catholics, meanwhile, invested legitimacy in the apostolic tradition, along with scripture as interpreted by the Church's hierarchy. A third issue concerned the number and operation of the sacraments, the rituals through which Christ communicates himself to his Church. Catholics identified seven sacraments, the efficacy of which depended on the proper conjunction of their form, matter, and participants' intent during their performance. Protestants recognized only two rites as sacraments—baptism and the Lord's Supper—tending (with much disagreement) to interpret their effectiveness spiritually. Protestants also declassified the clergy as a special caste mediating between God and the "priesthood of all believers"—the laity, who could now access God directly through the Bible.

Recent scholarship speaks of multiple reformations, rather than a single Reformation. Some featured alliances between commanding Protestant clerics and secular rulers. The paradigmatic figure was John Calvin, a lawyer turned Genevan pastor. Calvin both systematized Reformed Protestant theology, which disclosed a transcendent God who willed the fate of souls unable to save themselves, and organized a court to impose discipline in the church and moral order upon the town. His movement launched activists toting Bibles and tracts bearing its imprimatur from Scotland to Hungary, pressing its model of church–state cooperation. Rather different tendencies emerged from the radical Reformation, a welter of groups pushing scriptural interpretation beyond what even most Protestants considered appropriate. Anabaptists denied that the Bible warranted infant baptism, Anti-Trinitarians rejected claims that it upheld the three-part understanding of God's nature affirmed at Nicaea and subsequent councils, and Spiritualists refused to accept that it contained ultimate truth. Forced to rebrand itself, the Catholic Church inaugurated its own Counter-Reformation. The Council of Trent (1545–1563) dismissed Protestant critiques of Catholic doctrine while seeking to improve the clergy's education and pastoral performance. Other initiatives reorganized the Church's central government, sponsored new religious orders, commenced a worldwide evangelization campaign, and invigorated lay practice. Their theological quarrels notwithstanding, Protestants and Catholics shared similar aspirations to revitalize what each side regarded as the one Christian Church and to refresh its capacity to uphold social order.

Contemporaries were far less disposed than are modern historians to recognize congruities between the several reformations and were far more willing to assert the superiority of their versions with swords as well as pens. Wars of religion convulsed Europe for more than a century, feeding upon the inherited ideal that Christendom's peace and social order required religious uniformity. The presence of Jews, Muslims, and dissenting Christians had always frustrated that vision, but, in the sixteenth and seventeenth centuries, Jews to a great extent kept—and were kept—to themselves. Having been virtually expelled from Christendom after the *Reconquista*, Muslims—specifically, the Ottoman Turks occupying southeastern Europe—threatened its well-being only from without.

A more novel problem arose from the reforming clamor itself: how could princes protect the one true faith in the face of multiplying claimants? As slaughtering dissidents wholesale to achieve religious homogeneity became more clearly futile, politicians and diplomats patched solutions aimed to preserve peace, rather than secure a right to religious liberty. The Dutch Republic generally left dissenters alone, as did the Polish-Lithuanian Commonwealth for a time; France gradually tightened the screws before expelling its Protestants (the Huguenots) in 1685. The Peace of Augsburg (1555) allowed princes in the Holy Roman Empire to choose their subjects' religion: either Catholicism or Lutheranism. The Treaty of Westphalia (1648) approved a third alternative: Reformed Protestantism. After the blood dried, a new religious topography prevailed in Europe: the farther north and west one traveled, the more Protestants one would likely meet; and in every locale, one would encounter some new religious minority—Christians marooned among Christians—whose existence their rulers and neighbors abided, more or less.

The Reformation gestured toward the first century and marched toward the eighteenth. Protestants and Catholics alike claimed Christian antiquity's heritage. Protestants avowed that they had purged Catholic corruption and were reinstating the primitive church revealed in scripture; the Roman Church spun itself as the true upholder of apostolic tradition. In actuality, there was no going back. Consensus holds that the Reformation reoriented world history, though scholars dispute its legacy. It has been credited with promoting the "modern" world of capitalism, secularism, and science—byproducts most frequently attributed to Protestants' behaviors, attitudes, and ethics. Many historians, however, now contend both that the Reformation correlated with, rather than caused, such developments and that it is too simplistic to assume that Catholics were always retrograde and Protestants always progressive.

The Reformation's religious impacts can be grasped more readily. It divided Western Christendom against itself and multiplied the ways in which Christians understood God, their worship, and each other. The fact of Christian pluralism forced conversations about managing the new reality, some of which proposed that both church and state might prosper without either trying to impose religious uniformity. The Reformation also validated the laity's vocation, whether performed through Bible reading, spiritual exercises, or appeals to an inner light. It did not normalize a world in which Christians might worship God according to their own consciences without drawing either the state's wrath or compatriots' alarm, but it unveiled the possibilities.

The Enlightenment, ca. 1660–ca. 1800

The Enlightenment continued to reconstruct Western Christianity while simultaneously challenging it. It had little impact on the Eastern Orthodox churches, the result as much of political anxieties generated by the French Revolution as of theological distaste. A broad intellectual movement that swelled in the later seventeenth century and crested in the eighteenth, the Enlightenment swept through much of Europe. It took account of the post-Westphalian religious settlement and the rise of European overseas empires after 1500. The former development sought to reduce confessional warfare by accepting toleration; the latter increased Europeans' contact with indigenous and Asian cultures, encouraging an understanding that all human beings can know God through reason ("natural religion") and that truth might be found beyond Christianity. The Enlightenment extended the interest in human affairs promoted earlier by Renaissance humanism and by natural philosophy, which examined the natural world by means of observation, esoteric knowledge, and scripture. Its descendant, modern science, emerged alongside the Enlightenment as a distinctive methodology moored in empiricism, experimentation, and materialism, though even in 1800 practitioners' attention to religious perspectives had not dimmed entirely.

Contemporaries understood the Enlightenment as, preeminently, a new kind of philosophical inquiry, while much subsequent scholarship has construed it as, in one way or other, the core of "modernity." Specialists argue about whether or not it constituted a single phenomenon or if it nurtured liberal, humanitarian, and secular values as opposed to furthering authoritarianism, structures of social domination, and moral absolutism. Granting that its overlapping thought patterns sometimes elevated imagination or sentiment over reason and that it left mixed legacies, one might nevertheless consider it an international reform campaign that generally certified reason as the surest vehicle for obtaining knowledge. Its adherents avowed that the present is more enlightened than the past, sought to enlist the (reading) public in the cause of bettering the human condition, and derided bigotry, fanaticism, and superstition.

Some Enlightenment currents evinced great hostility toward organized belief, but most scholars now recognize a "religious Enlightenment," whose proponents included Jews as well as Protestants and Catholics. Religious Enlighteners attempted to rejuvenate their traditions by using science and philosophy to promote a tolerant faith that could serve a shared morality and politics. In Geneva, theologians muted Calvin's concept of predestination, stressing instead how Reformed Protestantism buttressed morality and obedience to civil rule. In central Europe, advocates of Reform Catholicism worked the new science and philosophy into university curricula and encouraged the Habsburg monarchy to assume greater control of the Church within its domains.

Whatever their specific programs, religious Enlighteners shared common concerns. Religion should be "reasonable," inhabiting the sweet spot between dogmatism, fanaticism, and skepticism. Revelation could augment reason, but could not contradict it. Conscience, they contended, obliges individuals to worship without state interference. Such arguments moved toleration into the religious mainstream, although in practice virtually everyone denied protection to one group or another. Many figures less sympathetic to religion embraced toleration as well; the French *philosophe* Voltaire blasted intolerance as ill-mannered, uncivilized, and contrary to good sense. This range of attacks mixed with continuing pragmatic acceptance of religious pluralism to corrode the assumption that civil stability requires religious uniformity.

The religious Enlightenment sought also to stabilize the biblical text. Such efforts began in the late seventeenth century, as both

Catholics and Protestants questioned scripture's reliability, authorship, chronologies, and language. Realizing that their canonical texts were becoming, as one contemporary put it, "strange, awkward, and new," eighteenth-century Protestants in England and Germany engineered techniques to parse it historically. Biblical scholars believed that shifting the basis of the Bible's authority from God's word to cultural analysis would uphold familiar Christian truths and keep skepticism at bay. But the larger project of radically rethinking the natural and supernatural worlds ultimately proved corrosive to pious certainties, especially when campaigns to reinstate religious uniformity and manage public morality inflamed opposition.

Deists posited a divinity whose being and laws reason could apprehend in nature and who, having created the world, no longer intervened in it. Exiled Huguenot philosopher Pierre Bayle unmoored morality from religion, arguing that atheists can behave as morally as Christians; Scottish skeptic David Hume propounded that ethics derive from each person's inherent moral sense, not church teaching. Inexorably, full-fledged atheism burst into view: coarsely in the anonymous *Treatise of the Three Imposters* (1719)—which impugned Moses, Jesus, and Muhammad for deceiving their devotees—and more elegantly in the philosophical materialism of the French *Encyclopédie*.

The Enlightenment also touched Jews, who had begun to filter back into central and western Europe. Rulers were sometimes willing to grant them substantial autonomy (if not full civil rights). Contacts with Christians exposed Jews to wider cultural and intellectual trends. Seventeenth-century Amsterdam housed a flourishing Jewish community, most of whom fitted themselves into rabbinic Judaism. Baruch Spinoza, a lens-grinder by trade and, more importantly, a philosophical virtuoso, proved a notable exception. Conceiving God as a force within nature, Spinoza denied that God works in history, that scripture is the revealed Word, and that the soul is immortal. Whether or not he

8. On the frontispiece of a late eighteenth-century French edition of *The Treatise of the Three Impostors*, a Jew, a Christian, and a Muslim hold masks, suggestive of their deceitfulness. This anonymous treatise excoriated Moses, Jesus, and Muhammad as tricksters who deluded their followers.

epitomized an antitheological and politically egalitarian "radical Enlightenment," however, he did not typify the Jewish Enlightenment (*Haskalah*), which aimed to reconstruct Judaism along rationalist lines, rather than deconstruct it altogether. Its leading figure, Moses Mendelssohn, advocated Jews' civil rights and their integration into European society. Translating the Pentateuch into German (written with Hebrew characters) and casting Judaism as a natural religion, he inspired other *maskilim* ("enlighteners") to promote the study of secular disciplines, straightforward explanations of Scripture, and the use of Hebrew in nonsacred writing. *Haskalah* eventually penetrated into eastern Europe, where many Jews repudiated its attacks on traditional education and calls to assimilate. Begun as an effort to reshape Judaism on rational grounds, *Haskalah* eventually turned to preparing Jews to align their values with the Enlightenment and assert their fitness to participate equally in European civil society.

The Enlightenment in its various guises launched a wholesale inquiry into humanity's relationship with God and nature; it celebrated, in philosopher Immanuel Kant's classic statement, the "freedom to make *public use* of one's reason in all matters." Completing what Protestant Reformers had begun, eighteenth-century lexicographers recast "religion" as belief and experience—personal piety—rather than merely the communal performance of ritual obligations. Taken together, these propositions elevated the authority of conscience and shifted the basic unit of religious identity from a community linked by practice and tradition to an individual who follows God according to one's own lights. Magistrates, philosophers, and religious minorities helped recalibrate the realms of civil and ecclesiastical control in favor of the former and extend the boundaries of toleration, finally endorsing religious liberty as a universal right. The religious Enlightenment's logic of natural religion conceptualized religion as a universal, autonomous category. The radical Enlightenment loosed genies of skepticism, doubt, and irreligion that have never been rebottled. Both impulses exposed religion to analytical dissection, with momentous consequences for Europe and, eventually, any realm exposed to Enlightenment values. No longer could Christianity—or any religious tradition—presume to structure society in its own image and likeness. Rather, all belief systems would be understood as discrete elements of human culture, rather than privileged sources of truth.

Movements of reform and renewal in Islam, ca. 1700–ca. 1900

Whereas the Reformation grew from slowly accreting but relatively recent concerns about the Church's direction, movements to refresh Islam drew on deeply embedded elements. The expectation that periodically a leader will revitalize the tradition by returning the *umma* to fundamentals—the Quran and the *Sunna*—derives from two seminal concepts: *islah* ("reform") and *tajdid* ("renewal"). Scholars have utilized a number of terms, including revivalism and fundamentalism, to classify movements seeking to enact programs based on these ideas; the usage here employs "reform" and "renewal" as near-synonyms designating a range of agendas springing from a common concern to recover root Islamic principles. *Islah* references the Quranic examples of reformer-prophets (especially Muhammad) who strove to increase their communities' righteousness. *Tajdid* is based on a *hadith* predicting the regular appearance of a religious "renewer" who will deploy *ijtihad* (independent judgment) to expunge perverting "innovations." As far back as the seventh-century Kharijites, Muslims concerned about alleged departures from tradition had launched campaigns to restore "authentic" Islam. The frequency of such efforts accelerated in the eighteenth and nineteenth centuries, catalyzed by the deteriorating political fortunes of the major Islamic polities, the perceived need to regularize Muslim practice in lands beyond the old Arab empire, and the spread of European colonialism.

The ideal of a unifying caliphate persisted long after the reality had disappeared. In Egypt the Mamluks appropriated the Abbasid claim in order to legitimate themselves but assumed the title "sultan" ("one with power"). Like caliphs, they defended Islam and patronized their *ulama*s. Three sultanates became politically and culturally dominant during the sixteenth and seventeenth centuries. Having in 1453 achieved the old Arab dream of capturing Byzantium—which they called Istanbul—the Ottoman Turks (r. 1299–1922) cast themselves as Islam's militant promoters, wrested the caliphate from the Mamluks, and constructed a cosmopolitan empire. Initially a Sufi (mystic) brotherhood that evolved into a band of holy warriors, the Safavid Dynasty (r. 1501–1722) remade Iran's religious profile, incrementally imposing Twelver Shiism via both carrots (promoting pilgrimages to Shiite shrines) and sticks (suppressing religious rivals). Facing a huge Hindu majority on the Indian subcontinent, Mughal emperors (r. 1526–1857) devised religious policies ranging from Akbar's cult of "divine religion," which recognized truth in all traditions, to Aurangzeb's enlistment of moral police to squash "un-Islamic" behavior. In the eighteenth century, the Ottomans retreated before the Habsburg and Russian empires, the Safavids fell to Afghan Sunnis grown restive under Shiite rule, and the Mughals ceded ground to local opponents and the British Empire.

Meanwhile, Islam reached into sub-Saharan Africa as well as south, central, and southeast Asia, imported by merchants, travelers, wandering scholars, and especially Sufi orders, whose religious eclecticism and charitable inclinations attracted converts to versions of Islam often suffused with non-Muslim rituals and beliefs. Movements of Islamic reform sprang from and reflected these disparate circumstances. Although they all urged social and moral transformations, they took different courses depending on how deeply Islam had entered the culture. Where mainstream Islamic customs were already the norm, reform movements tried primarily to eliminate departures from well-established practice;

where customs were still somewhat hybridized, they strove to form putatively traditional Islamic societies. In the eighteenth century, they tended to emerge primarily from local Islamic concerns, while in the nineteenth, they increasingly involved resistance to European expansion and ideas.

Within the context of reasserting *tawhid* (God's oneness), launching harsh critiques against popular practices and institutions, and calibrating *ijtihad*'s scope, renewal programs took different stands. Muhammad Ibn abd al-Wahhab led the most prominent campaign. Disparaging such customs as shrine visitations and charging his followers to reject anything deemed to deflect attention from God, he joined with Muhammad ibn Saud, a tribal chief, to forge a renewalist alliance. The Saudi state conquered most of the Arabian Peninsula, destroying Sufi, Shiite, and even Sunni holy sites before the Ottomans overwhelmed it for threatening their rule. Reform proceeded otherwise in contemporary Iran, where a prolonged debate among Shiite jurists over the legitimacy of using *ijtihad* to issue legal rulings in the Hidden Imam's absence ended with victory for those who affirmed that the practice was valid.

A reform current might change trajectory over time. In south Asia, for instance, Shah Wali Allah, a leading intellectual, mediated between Sunni law schools and argued for extending *ijtihad* to the larger *umma*. As Mughal power ebbed, his son, Abd al-Aziz, assumed a more militant stance, declaring that an India ruled by Britain no longer belonged to *Dar al-Islam* and exhorting Muslims to flee or fight. Al-Aziz's student Sayyid Ahmad Barelwi condemned practices he regarded as contaminated by Sufi, Shiite, or Hindu customs; he died conducting *jihad* against the Sikhs. Occasionally renewalism took a messianic turn. Declaring himself to be the Mahdi—God's appointed restorer of true Islam and divine justice—Muhammad Ahmad conducted *jihad* against the Ottoman Egyptians, setting up a Sudanese state that lasted until an Anglo-Egyptian army dispatched it in 1898. In Iran, a previously Shiite sect evolved under the teachings of Bahaullah into the Baha'i Faith, a new religion preaching the unity of God, the essential identity of all prophets' messages, and the singleness of humanity.

Another approach emerged in the later nineteenth century, by which time Christian Europe's extensive colonization of Muslim societies, as well as its apparent superiority in politics, economics, science, and war, seemed to threaten Islam morally and even existentially. Small cadres of "modernist" intellectuals determined that Muslims themselves bore extensive blame for having followed legal rulings robotically. While supporting a return to Quran and *Sunna*, they discerned some virtue in European values and institutions. They deployed *ijtihad*—by which they meant "critical thinking"—to recruit Western modes of thought and action in order to promote Islam's vitality and Muslims' independence. Jamal al-Din al-Afghani, a journalist and political activist, pressed Muslims to reclaim their scientific heritage, advocated parliamentary forms of government, and urged *ijtihad* as the means of achieving political liberation.

His student Muhammad Abduh, Egypt's chief judge of *Sharia*, crafted a theory of reform, Salafism, that extolled the "Pious Ancestors" (*al-salaf al-salih*)—the early *umma*, in his view—for having actualized Muhammad's revelation. Abduh encouraged Muslims to emulate their forbears' creative example by renewing the tradition through *ijtihad* and accepting elements of Western culture, if appropriate. In India Sir Sayyid Ahmad Khan founded what is now Aligarh Muslim University. Islamic modernism cast concepts of parliamentary government and scientific methods into Islamic idioms, argued for extending *ijtihad* beyond the *ulama*, and laid out pathways for renovating Muslim societies, but it did not develop organizational structures capable of effecting large-scale change.

The fact that reform and renewal in Islam have taken disparate forms should come as no surprise, given its decentralized institutions. Unlike Protestants, Sunni reformers had no prevailing entity like the Catholic Church against which to define and distinguish themselves. Modernists' disdain for the *ulama* recalls Protestants' contempt for Catholic clergy, but most reformers disavowed that path. Political contexts and the magnitude of European intervention in Muslim societies mattered too. Although most eighteenth- and nineteenth-century renewal movements had impacts on regional Muslim communities rather than on the *umma* globally, they collectively laid templates for the future. The most influential was (and is) the one founded by al-Wahhab, who preached an austere, exclusivist brand of Islam that condemned anything that strayed from its allegedly "pure" seventh-century form. Wahhabism rebounded in the twentieth century alongside a resurgent Saudi state that used its newfound oil fortune to project Wahhabi ideology—infused with a conservative strain of Salafism that defined the "Pious Ancestors" in more restrictive terms than had Abduh and that renounced Western thought—around the world. Modernism, albeit a minority preserve, advanced a platform of critical self-reflection conjoined with respect for tradition that has inspired contemporary "progressive Muslim" calls for religious inclusivism and social justice.

Reforming Judaism (ca. 1750–ca. 1900)

History and tradition ushered reform within Judaism down a very different path. Two conditions had configured Jewish life for nearly 2,000 years. Sociologically, Jews had constituted a distinctive religious community subordinated within foreign polities. Religiously, they had reconstructed their tradition around the pillars of rabbinic leadership and the dual (Oral and Written) Torah. For over a millennium, acceptance of these foundations had resulted in a mainstream Judaism with beliefs and practices that might vary over time and place, but adherents had neither the basis nor need to imagine religious reform in terms analogous to *islah* and *tajdid*. Pressures to rethink how Jews lived and practiced their faith erupted, however, in late eighteenth- and nineteenth-century Europe. Jews had ordinarily lived in semiautonomous and often insular enclaves, experiencing intermittent contact with Gentile neighbors and exercising little power beyond their own communities. Now, as Europeans reorganized themselves politically into nation-states that defined their populations as individual citizens rather than as a ruler's subjects, they began to emancipate the Jews, offering them an unparalleled chance at full social integration—if they understood themselves as citizens first, Jews second.

This opportunity collided, however, with the demands of tradition and its hard-wired presumption that Judaism and Jewishness composed an integrated whole that could not be separated into religious, cultural, or national identities. Citizenship tore at Jews' sense of belonging to *Am Yisrael*, a single body dedicated to Torah and *halakhah*, rather than forming merely an association of individual "Israelites." Some converted to Christianity or let their worship lapse, but the majority, for whom tradition still mattered, had to determine for themselves how they were still Jews while simultaneously signaling to their neighbors that they were fellow citizens distinguishable only by having chosen Judaism rather than Christianity as their religion. The answers emerged in central and western Europe, home to a minority of the continent's Jews, including its wealthiest and most educated.

The initial response reflected the desire of some German Jews to make worship more attractive and meaningful, while demonstrating to Christians that Jewish ritual was both decorous and rational. Reformers tinkered with the liturgy by expanding the time for sermons, introducing choirs of men and women accompanied by an organ, and reciting prayers in German. By the 1840s, these moves had escalated into a more sweeping program. Rabbi Abraham Geiger articulated Reform Judaism's cardinal premises most clearly. Judaism, he said, is a religion, a category distinct from culture or nationality. Jewish tradition has changed constantly; its sacred texts are not timeless revelations, but historically conditioned sources available to update that tradition. This framework generated further propositions. The Talmud reflects the Judaism of its day and holds no special religious authority for the present. Israel is no longer a nation but a religious community; it expects no Messiah but affirms its mission to establish a messianic age of truth, justice, and peace.

Reform Judaism took root most strongly in the United States, where Jews adopted it as much from a desire to fit into American culture as from theological commitment. Free from government interference and much of Europe's anti-Semitism, Reformers in the United States organized a denomination with congregational and clerical institutions. In 1885, a rabbinic assembly propounded Reform's consummate nineteenth-century exposition, the Pittsburgh Platform, which emphasized the universality of Judaism's ethics and declared that the laws regulating diet and ritual purity "fail to impress the modern Jew with a spirit of priestly holiness."

But a backlash had already begun among traditionalist Jews who defended what they considered to be orthodox (correct) practice. Some of them, repulsed by any effort to accommodate to modern life, insisted that custom as well as performing *halakhah* meticulously meant segregating themselves from everyone else, including Jews with whom they disagreed. Most, however, followed the course of Rabbi Samson Raphael Hirsch, who conceded Jewish integration into Gentile society under terms that, he maintained, kept the tradition of dual Torah inviolate. Averring that *halakhah* is divinely ordained and that the Torah's ordinances must be accepted in their entirety, Hirsch nonetheless allowed some liturgical changes, education in secular subjects, and practices such as wearing clothes undistinguishable from what non-Jews wore. Defining Israel as a holy people charged with teaching about God who await the Messiah, Orthodox Judaism claimed to be the true, eternal faith that had existed since the revelation at Sinai.

A third movement, tracing back to Rabbi Zecharias Frankel, mediated between Reform and Orthodoxy, adapting the former's world view and the latter's practices. Frankel granted the premise that Judaism had changed over time, but contended that the findings of Jewish historical scholarship justified obeying the Oral Law (in line with Orthodoxy) even though it was a human creation (in line with Reform). Conservative Judaism—the American denominational realization of what began as Germany's "positive-historical" school—held that Israel is a people with a particular religious and ethnic identity who might live among others. It retained belief in the Messiah, the importance of observing *halakhah*, and a liturgical preference for Hebrew.

Orthodox and Conservative Jews distinguished themselves in opposition to Reform, but the three movements were equally products of their time, wrestling with their identities as both *Am Yisrael* and citizens of a nation-state. Each appealed to history to prove that its Judaism alone authentically represented tradition. Among Ashkenazic Jewry (broadly, the culture complex radiating from the medieval Rhineland), these inventions of "Judaism"—particularly the choice of some Orthodox Jews to live in self-isolating communities—fragmented the sense of common peoplehood into greater sectarian division and mutual contentiousness than Jews had experienced since the time of the Second Temple. Sephardic Jewry (broadly, the culture complex originating in medieval Iberia) drew no such internal boundaries.

Reform in the Abrahamic religions

The contexts and ideologies that shaped reform in Judaism, Christianity, and Islam are sufficiently different that no comprehensive typology is likely to be useful, although one can note similarities, most of which result from parallel evolution. Islamic modernists invoked the Protestant Reformation as an inspiration, though they often cast Luther as a "latter-day Muslim." Opening *ijtihad* to the whole Islamic community (the *umma*) betrays an impulse similar to—if historically separate from—exposing scripture to the mass of Christian faithful (the priesthood of all believers). Scholars of the religious Enlightenment often overlook Islamic modernism, but its program justifies including it as an indigenous Muslim variant. Protestantism and Islamic renewalism share a primal—if separately generated—urge to base their truths on founding authorities. *Haskalah* emerged from the religious Enlightenment; Reform Judaism followed in its wake.

Nevertheless, reform movements—like so much in the Abrahamic religions—have also borne the impress of their differing political contexts. Throughout much of their histories, Christians, Muslims, and Jews have imagined their traditions as informing the totality of their existence, rather than as composing a single aspect of their lives. The Reformation and Enlightenment, which rattled such constructions, arose in Western Christian polities, whose inhabitants contended on their own terms about what place to accord Christianity culturally and politically. They had little cause to consider how their experiments might function in non-Christian sovereignties.

Islamic reformers of all stripes, by contrast, operated in the twilight of Islam's imperium. Frequently subject to foreign rule, they promoted moral rejuvenation as a prerequisite for Muslims to reclaim power while restoring Islam to its full place in society. Jewish reform, meanwhile, arose among populations whose lived Judaism had gone hand in hand with political subordination, but who were now being incorporated into European civil society on uniquely liberal terms. That shock prompted reassessments of received tradition even among those most committed to preserving it. Unlike virtually all Islamic and Christian reform movements, which guarded the authority of their customary sources, Reform Judaism dared to re-evaluate one of its pillars—the Oral Law—and, as it did, redefined *Am Yisrael* to conform with the modern secular state's expectations of its citizens. In this light, at least, nineteenth-century Reform Judaism might be considered the most radical reform movement among the Abrahamic religions.

Chapter 7
Modern encounters
(1500-2010)

After 1500, Christianity became the preeminent religion in many of the world's most powerful nations, facilitating its global spread. The recovery of political sovereignty by Muslims in Asia and Africa following decolonization in the twentieth century resulted in reassertions of Islam's foundational importance for political cultures in those regions. Meanwhile, world Jewry reorganized itself primarily in Israel and the United States, a state that officially promoted no religion while proclaiming itself to be culturally Christian yet also committed to protecting religious liberty. As disagreements between Jews, Christians, and Muslims continued, some sought to increase harmony among them by launching global theological initiatives.

The global expansion of Christianity (ca. 1500-2010)

In 1500, Christians lived almost exclusively in Europe. In 2010, an estimated 2.2 billion Christians—the most adherents of any religion—lived around the world, with the largest concentrations in the Americas, Europe, and sub-Saharan Africa. Western Christianity's global reach drew on two tendencies—proselytizing and consorting with state power—that the Eastern Orthodox Church did not mobilize as effectively. Catholicism and Protestantism gained from being quartered alongside European imperialism's launching pads, although the relationship between the Gospel's spread and the continent's empire-building was complex. Economic and geopolitical motives drove empire, although expressions about saving souls (and uplifting backward peoples) often justified territorial expansion. The sword might open the way of the cross, but so too might cargo ships.

Where empires planted permanent colonies, migrants carried the faith, with clergy hoping to recruit the indigenes sometimes leading the way and sometimes trailing behind. Elsewhere, Christian growth depended on missionaries alone. They might serve an imperial enterprise directly, but more usually they operated under ecclesiastical rather than civil auspices. Some missionaries took economic advantage of their charges; others tried to protect them from exploitation. The ability to create sustained Christian communities primarily by conversion depended on such factors as the level at which resident elites opposed or supported missionary activity, the benefits—material as well as spiritual—that conversion seemed to offer indigenous peoples, the extent to which European clergy allowed native acolytes to assume full clerical responsibilities, and the degree to which native converts imported their own practices and beliefs into the liturgy and Christian devotional life.

The Catholic Church moved first, mounting a concerted evangelization effort across the sixteenth through eighteenth centuries. Propelled by the imperial projects of Spain, Portugal, and France, it marshaled numerous religious orders, especially the Jesuits. By far the greatest expansion occurred in Central and South America, where conquest of the aboriginal peoples, greatly abetted by epidemic disease, opened the Western Hemisphere to large-scale Catholic migration. Simultaneously, Franciscan friars staffing scores of mission compounds systematically converted the *Indios*, integrating them economically and religiously into Spanish colonial society as a subordinate caste.

In Asia, dense populations, natives' devotion to their inherited traditions, hostile rulers, and disputes among competing orders dogged most efforts to introduce Christianity. The growth of small but committed communities fashioned by Jesuits' creative folding of native customs into church life encountered stifling challenges: papal denunciations—incited by rival missionaries—that converts maintained "heathen" practices (India, China); political backlash against the Church (China); and massive persecution (Japan). The Church achieved its one unalloyed Asian success in the Philippines, where its tactics mimicked those in the Americas. Spain claimed the islands for itself, the Spanish Crown supported the clergy's efforts, and evangelization proceeded alongside the organization of *encomiendas*, estates on which the colonizers could take over native Filipinos' goods and labor.

Elsewhere, the Church struggled. Initially promising ventures in Portuguese Kongo and East Africa ebbed by the eighteenth century for reasons including civil war and the slave trade, which tarred Christianity as the religion of body-snatchers. The Church had little opportunity for and less interest in attracting Muslims, though missionaries fortified its presence in Hungary and adjoining Ottoman provinces. Rome's efforts waned by 1800, sapped by the Catholic empires' decline, the papacy's suppression of the Jesuits (for reasons having to do with European politics, not missions), and the French Revolution, though by then the faith had secured centers of gravity outside Europe, especially Latin America. The Church never ceased its missionary activities, though in the nineteenth century its apostles more readily revived settled flocks than created new ones.

Eighteenth-century Protestants had undertaken scattered ventures; most notably, Danish Lutherans nestled missions among India's Tamils, and the Moravian Brethren—an offshoot of the fifteenth-century Bohemian church—reached African slaves in the Caribbean and Indians in Anglo-America. The nineteenth century registered a change in magnitude as British missionaries, flush with abolitionist sentiment, enthusiasm for improving natives' lot, and attachment to the world's most powerful empire, took up the imperial dream of promoting Anglophone civilization worldwide. American and continental Protestants followed. Yet despite some local success among lower-caste and aboriginal groups, India frustrated Protestant hopes. Expectations crashed against imperial officials' concern not to rile native religious sensibilities, along with proselytizers' difficulties navigating the caste system. Missionaries also made no inroads among Middle Eastern Muslims, though they sporadically stimulated spirituality among some Eastern Christians.

The one bright spot in East Asia was Korea, where Protestantism (and Catholicism) spread through homegrown activism and came to embody national resistance to foreign powers (notably Japan), rather than humiliation by them. In the western Pacific, British and Irish settlers established Protestantism and Catholicism; local chieftains found it politically advantageous to curry favor from one or another missionary, and traveling islanders spread the Gospel spontaneously. Protestants fared well in sub-Saharan Africa through a complicated process that owed less to missionaries than to the agency with which Africans reshaped Christianity into a vehicle for opposing European hegemony and asserting their own self-worth. The real jewel in the crown, however, lay in another hemisphere, where British colonists planted a mixed multitude of denominations in a land destined to become the world's largest Protestant bastion: the United States.

By 1900, if not earlier, Christianity had become a more extensive world religion than had Islam, aided by the spread of global empires and commercial networks from its European stronghold. Outside parts of Africa, it had not done so by winning head-to-head competitions. Christians made few converts even in the Muslim lands they controlled, but, in bypassing *Dar al-Islam* for even more distant lands, they exported the faith to realms that had been largely unaware of the Abrahamic religions.

Religion and politics in modern Muslim states (ca. 1900–2010)

In 1500, Muslims could be found across Africa and Eurasia, from the Strait of Gibraltar to the Strait of Malacca, from Madagascar to the Caucasus. In 2010 the great bulk of the world's estimated 1.6 billion Muslims—the second-largest body of religious adherents—remained in historically Islamic territory. A majority of them, 61.8 percent, lived in Asia beyond the Middle East, 19.8 percent in the Middle East and North Africa, and 15.5 percent in sub-Saharan Africa; they had also begun moving into Europe and the Americas. Muslims' return to Western societies occurred as they pondered how to construct a new Islamic political order within their traditional domains. The Ottoman Empire's dismemberment following World War I and colonialism's demise after World War II meant that *Dar al-Islam* now consisted of more than fifty distinct and economically underdeveloped nation-states whose boundaries had been largely drawn and maintained by the receding imperial powers.

Muslims had long debated how to construct Islam as an all-consuming worldview and the *umma* as a universal entity. The postcolonial reality confronted them with a conundrum about calibrating Muslim and civic identities. How could (and should) the new polities incorporate Islam while erecting both governance structures whose nationalist principles demanded citizens' primary loyalty and economies whose viability presupposed accepting secular models? Colonialism's legacy also had significant implications for *Sharia*, which had changed from being a community-based legal system, in which the *ulama* might restrain the ruler, into a politicized instrument that the state could implement. Interpretations of Islam figured in subsequent discussions about nation-building, but the ways in which Muslims reworked religion into politics were anything but uniform.

For much of the twentieth century, nearly all newly independent Muslim-majority states foregrounded secular ideologies, while referencing Islam as a common religious heritage or source of law. One noteworthy exception was Saudi Arabia, established in 1932. The House of Saud enlisted its longtime Wahhabi clerical allies to staff the state *Sharia* courts and legitimize their rule. At the other extreme, Mustafa Kemal Atatürk transformed the Ottoman Empire's heartland into the Republic of Turkey, which disestablished Islam and in 1924 abolished the caliphate.

In general, states deployed Islam for their own particular purposes. During the 1950s and '60s, Egypt's Gamal Abd al-Nasser championed socialism, pan-Arabism, and economic development, cultivating support by nationalizing al-Azhar University and soliciting *fatwa*s from its *ulama*. From 1957 to 1998, Indonesia, the most populous Muslim nation, was headed by two presidents who circumscribed the activities of Islamic parties and promoted a nationalist ideology, *Pancasila* ("Five Principles"); its first tenet—belief in one God (not Allah by name)—struck numerous Muslims as un-Islamic. In Pakistan—constituted as a parliamentary democracy that prohibited laws contrary to the Quran and *Sunna*—the first three administrations (1956–88) wielded Islam to support successively liberal-modernist, socialist, and religiously conservative platforms. By the late 1960s and 1970s, however, mounting economic underperformance, social instability, political malfeasance, and military shocks—especially Israel's capture of Jerusalem in 1967—had broadly discredited secularism, leading many Muslims to reaffirm Islam as intrinsic to their political and cultural identities.

This turn toward reintegrating politics into an all-inclusive Islamic way of life had been presaged by two earlier renewal movements: the Muslim Brotherhood, founded in Egypt by Hasan al-Banna in 1928, and *Jamaat-i-Islami* (the Islamic Society), begun in India by Sayyid Abu al-Ala al-Mawdudi in 1941. Organized originally as communities of religious activists, the

Brotherhood and *Jamaat* sought to re-Islamize their societies by running educational, charitable, and social-welfare programs or training committed Muslim leaders, respectively. Rejecting nationalism, the politics (if not necessarily the intellectual substance) of Islamic modernism, and hidebound legal traditionalism, they insisted that Islam is a self-sufficient system capable of accommodating the modern world on its own terms.

Moves to "re-Islamize" society and politics have taken different courses. Arguably the most momentous occurred in Shiite Iran. In 1979, an uprising that came to be dominated by followers of Ayatollah Ruhollah Khomeini overthrew Reza Shah Pahlavi, whose earlier "White Revolution" had exemplified Western modernization. The resulting Islamic Republic took unique form: elected officials served under a supreme leader who, in line with Khomeini's highly controversial doctrine of *vilayat-i faqih* ("regency of the jurist"), ruled with the Hidden Imam's divine authority.

Less dramatic but far more widespread was Islam's political and social normalization within mainstream civil society. For example, despite being frequently harassed and jailed, members of the Muslim Brotherhood increasingly participated in Egyptian electoral politics, pressing for the implementation of *Sharia* law and ultimately forming their own party. Under Recep Tayyip Erdogan, first elected prime minister in 2003, Turkey's Justice and Development Party increased Islam's public identification with the state by, for instance, allowing women serving in educational institutions, the police, and the military to wear head scarves.

These "quiet revolutions" were, however, frequently upstaged in public perceptions by radical Islamists, cadres who in their own minds represented the global *umma*, rather than a particular nation-state. They interpreted *jihad* as license to establish God's law by any means necessary, including violence against any opponent, Muslim or non-Muslim. Their foremost ideological godfather was Sayyid Qutb, a Muslim Brother executed by Nasser. Qutb excoriated anyone he deemed incapable of carrying out Islam's "inalienable right" to establish itself as a "universal and human religion." To advance this cause, radical Islamists deployed terror and bloodshed, most spectacularly in al-Qaeda's demolition of the World Trade Center on September 11, 2001, and rather more grindingly in the efforts of the Islamic State in Iraq and the Levant (ISIL, aka ISIS) to restore the caliphate. Viewed within Islamic history's sweep, jihadists might be understood not only as heralding Islam's expansion, but also as rehearsing a script as old as the Umayyads and Kharijites: using religion to legitimize—or delegitimize—Muslim regimes. From this perspective, radical Islam is an extremist minority's exercise in *ijtihad*.

The reconfiguration of world Jewry (ca. 1500–2010)

In 1500, many Jews were heading toward one of two domains. The first was the Ottoman Empire, which especially welcomed Sephardic Jews skilled in commerce and diplomacy. Speaking Ladino (Spanish inflected with Turkish and other tongues), the Sephardim revitalized Jewish communities like the Galilean town of Safed. There, the sixteenth-century rabbi Isaac Luria taught a type of Kabbalistic mysticism that connected Jews' suffering with God's imperfections, stressing their collective capacity to effect the Godhead's restoration and ring in the messianic age. Luria influenced Shabbetai Zevi, who thrilled Ottoman and eastern European Jews by proclaiming himself the Messiah in the mid-seventeenth century. Zevi's movement outlived him even though—facing execution for threatening the sultan—he converted to Islam.

The other hub was eastern Europe—primarily Poland and Lithuania—which accepted Jewish refugees to increase trade and manage nobles' estates. By the eighteenth century, it housed 80 percent of the world's Jews. Sequestered in villages and *shtetls* (market towns), they spoke Yiddish (German spiced with Hebrew and Slavic idioms), dutifully followed custom, and practiced another form of Kabbalah, which served them less as a cosmic guide than as applied magic. Within this milieu wandered folk healers boasting access to divine powers. The greatest was the *Hasid* ("Pious One") Israel ben Eliezer; called the Baal Shem Tov ("Master of the Good Name"), he elevated ecstatic experience over study and *halakhic* observance. His disciples organized communities around charismatic rabbis, who claimed to intercede with God on their followers' behalf. Hasidism eventually came to represent an extremely traditionalist version of modern Orthodox Judaism. Meanwhile, it drew fire from the *mitnagdim* ("opponents"), rabbis deeply committed to Talmudic study and suspicious of Hasidic antinomianism. Their champion was Elijah ben Solomon Zalman, the "Vilna Gaon." Renowned for his piety and intellect, the Gaon stressed learning Torah for its own sake, a discipline that stimulated the formation of the dedicated educational institutions called yeshivas.

As always, Jews' status fluctuated according to circumstances. The Ottomans regulated *dhimmi*s benignly at first, but military setbacks, economic stagnation, and the resulting anxiety fostered harsher treatment of minorities. Poland-Lithuania's tolerationist regime afforded Jews considerable security—until Ukrainian Cossacks massacred them during a revolt against Polish rule in 1648. Austria, Prussia, and Russia carved up the Polish state between 1772 and 1795, after which Russia confined Jews to the "Pale of Settlement" inside its western borders for more than a century. Jews' formal standing elsewhere improved markedly in the nineteenth century, as virtually all European nations—and Muslim ones pressed by European powers to protect Christians and Jews—granted them civil equality. Nevertheless, widespread hostility against Jews continued. Their position worsened in Russia, where czarist hostility and popularly led pogroms compounded economic decline; in the Levant and Maghreb, where their embrace of Western mores enflamed Muslims, who linked them with colonialism; and even in western and central Europe, where the definition of nations as ethnic units, rather than civic associations, presumed that Jews could never belong. Discontent and frustration drove a portion of eastern European Jews into socialist movements, but a far greater number migrated to the United States between 1880 and 1920, making it home to the world's largest Jewish community.

Perhaps the most creative response came from Theodor Herzl, a journalist who dismissed both the Enlightenment's premise that Jews were a religious community and its promise of equal citizenship. Jews were a nation needing a homeland, he argued, and he founded a movement—Zionism—to establish one. For nearly two millennia, Jews had dreamed of restoring the Temple in Jerusalem, but Zionism was—despite a minor strain exhorting return to the "Holy Land"—fundamentally secular. Zionists disagreed about many things—including, initially, where to locate the homeland—but they soon decided on Palestine.

Jews' deteriorating conditions were underwritten by anti-Semitism, which reimagined an ancient enmity. In the past, Christians and Muslims had dismissed Judaism as a deficient faith, while Jew-haters had assailed Jews' "alien" customs, economic "advantages," or "malign" character. Debunking the liberal claim that Jews differed from others merely by virtue of their religious practice, anti-Semites cast them as an innately debased "nation" that poisoned "civilized" society from within. Racial anti-Semitism culminated in the Holocaust (*ha-Shoah*, "destruction"), the Nazis' extermination of six million Jews. Zionist migration to Palestine had begun in the late nineteenth century, but the Holocaust, the ensuing surge of refugees, and Britain's cession of Palestine (which it had governed since the Ottoman Empire's fall) led the United Nations to partition the area into Jewish and Arab states. After declaring independence in 1948, Israel repulsed a multilateral Arab invasion. Finding themselves both on hostile ground, Jews bolted from Arab lands, often under duress, while some 750,000 Palestinians fled or were expelled from their homes.

These events had massive consequences. The creation of Israel—the first Jewish sovereignty in the region since Hasmonean Judea vanished in the first century BCE—further roiled Middle Eastern politics. Israelis and their allies extolled the "Jewish state" as a liberal democracy and a sanctuary for Jews worldwide. But most Muslims regarded the "Zionist entity" as a vestige of Western imperialism that oppressed the native Palestinians. Disagreements over manifold issues incited ongoing violence on all sides. Israel's existence also stirred religious feelings. Among Jews, religious Zionists considered its creation a key step toward realizing the messianic age of national redemption. For Christian Zionists, it testified to God's continuing covenant with the Jewish people and satisfied a necessary condition for Christ's Second Coming. Muslims, who regard Jerusalem as Islam's third holiest site, resented restrictions barring Palestinians and others from entering the Al-Aqsa mosque, thereby hindering their duty to maintain it.

By 2010, Jews escaping persecution had once again gathered themselves into two large blocks, a rather different pair than what had existed a half-millennium earlier. Their existence in Muslim territory and eastern Europe had essentially vanished, with 41.1 percent (5.7 million) living in the United States and 40.5 percent in Israel, although, by 2015, some estimates had vaulted Israel's percentage into the lead. But their overall numbers had thinned; a global population of perhaps 14 million had not yet recovered its pre–World War II figure. Unlike Christians—87 percent of whom lived in Christian-majority countries—or Muslims—73 percent of whom inhabited *Dar al-Islam*—only a minority lived in a Jewish-majority state. This demography reflected Jews' historical experience: they seldom proselytized or held state power, two activities conducive to enlarging one's religious community.

Jews and Muslims in Christian America
(ca. 1600–2010)

How Jews, Christians, and Muslims interacted with each other always depended on the political environment. In the United States, their collective experiences were shaped by constitutional and cultural arrangements that evolved after independence to guide the interface between religion and politics. The new American nation overthrew the European ideal of a confessional state, which preferred, or even demanded, that its subjects belong to one church. Instead, it instigated a dynamic in which Christianity was integral to American identity, even though the national state privileged no single sect. The Federal Constitution (1787) and the First Amendment (1791) eliminated religious requirements for holding national office, forbade Congress from creating ecclesiastical establishments, and enshrined religion's free exercise. The individual states likewise protected religious liberty, though many of them initially restricted non-Protestants from obtaining full citizenship, and three kept their church establishments into the nineteenth century. Drawing upon classical antiquity, British history, and the Anglo-American colonies' experience of self-government, the Constitution built a formally secular national state.

Nonetheless, virtually all Americans at the nation's founding agreed with President George Washington that "religion and morality are indispensable supports" of "political prosperity." They were almost all Protestants, although fewer than 20 percent actually joined churches as members, and no denomination prevailed nationwide. They also understood religious liberty as a person's right to worship God as his or her conscience dictates, a stance validated by both Protestantism's esteem for individual Bible-reading and the Enlightenment's endorsement of natural religion. Acknowledging this individual liberty did not, however, guarantee public acceptance of any particular religious body.

Under these conditions, religious groups did not enjoy formal constitutional advantages over each other, but they could still vie for political power and cultural authority. No longer eligible for state support, Protestants engineered revivals and voluntary associations to proselytize and promote social agendas. Collectively, they strove to limit other Christians' influence. Their robust hatred of "popery" tarred Catholics as Roman agents who would destroy American democracy if allowed to control the government. By legislating their ethics into law, Protestants could circumvent the prohibition against church establishments. Congress delayed Utah's statehood until its Mormon majority abandoned the doctrine of plural marriage. Moreover, no constitutional provision forbade unofficially contriving the United States as a Christian nation, although what "Christian" meant (other than statistically) was a matter of debate. Some Christian nationalists declared American republican institutions to be consonant with the Bible and the United States, like ancient Israel, to have entered into a covenant with God.

Yet the interplay of religion and politics in American life was never static. A Catholic won the presidency in 1960, Protestants had lost their majority status in the population by 2010, and legislation promoting Christian morality often failed or was repealed. Minorities have enjoyed religious liberty in the United States, but they must still navigate shifting political and cultural contingencies that affect how the still-Christian majority judges whether their behavior comports with their perceived "fitness" to be citizens socially and culturally as well as politically.

The first Jews to settle in what would become the United States were a handful of Sephardim escaping Brazil for Dutch New Amsterdam in 1654. During the American Revolution, Jews overwhelmingly supported independence, facilitating their integration into the new republic. Three migrations configured American Jewry. The first (1820–1860) brought tens of thousands of German-speakers and their inclinations toward Reform

Judaism. The next (1880–1920) added millions of eastern European Ashkenazim and amplified traditionalist perspectives. A third, which included German intellectuals fleeing anti-Semitism in the 1930s and Hasids quitting Europe after the Holocaust, boosted American Jews' religious diversity further. So did Reconstructionism, a homegrown movement that defined Judaism as a "civilization" instead of a religion or ethnicity.

American Jews endured state-level civil restrictions into the nineteenth century; ostracism from certain careers, social organizations, and schools well into the twentieth; and sporadic violence throughout both centuries. Nevertheless, they never suffered widespread physical abuse, and in the mid-twentieth century public attitudes toward them improved, reflecting acceptance of what President-elect Dwight Eisenhower called the "Jud[e]o-Christian concept," which supposed that Judaism shares basic truths with Protestantism and Roman Catholicism. Although theologically suspect, this notion enlisted Jews as equals with Christian Americans in upholding God and democracy against fascism and communism. The American Jewish community proved distinctive, most importantly because conditions within the American diaspora were unparalleled. Since the Babylonian captivity, diasporic Jews had usually lived as discrete (and subordinate) communities that identified more readily with Jews beyond their own borders than with their non-Jewish neighbors. By the late twentieth century, American Jews could affirm that they belonged fully to both *Am Yisrael* and the United States.

The first Muslims came to Anglo-America as slaves imported from West Africa. Anecdotes about people kneeling to pray on a mat testify to their observing traditional Islamic worship practices as long as they could. Slaves' inability to build permanent institutions, however, along with nineteenth-century masters' drive to Christianize them, helped extinguish Islam's early traces. Homegrown varieties such as the Nation of Islam, which mixed

Islamic symbolism with black nationalism, offered African Americans fleeing the Jim Crow South a spirituality divorced from whites' Christianity. Although much of the Nation of Islam eventually moved toward mainstream Sunnism, "black Islam" was unanchored in fundamental Islamic principles and had little resonance among other Muslims. Historically traditional forms of Islam again reached the United States around 1870 to 1914, when Arabic-speaking immigrants sought homesteads or factory jobs in the Midwest, but they too failed to create a national Islamic "infrastructure." The Immigration Act of 1965, which lifted restrictions on non-European migrants, transformed the American Muslim population. Subsequently, middle-class professionals and their families seeking economic and educational advancement entered the United States from South Asia and Africa as well as the Middle East, pushing the American Muslim population to 2.8 million in 2010. Their numbers and growing wealth helped construct composite identities: part American, part American Muslim, and part member of the global *umma*.

The diversity and preponderantly foreign origins of American Muslims in the early twenty-first century posed puzzles. They had to learn how to fund mosques without state support and to apply Islamic law to questions raised by their status outside *Dar al-Islam* while simultaneously adjudicating between different legal schools. The degree of animosity they faced intensified dramatically after 9/11. Fueled more by politics than religious difference, it manifested itself in government surveillance as well as personal attacks. American Muslims faced the same questions about their capacity to be trustworthy American citizens that had earlier confronted Catholics, Mormons, and Jews.

Ambivalent relationships (ca. 1900–2010)

The modern world may have brought Jews, Christians, and Muslims into repeatedly close contact, but proximity at times bred only contempt. Polemics continued, inflected, as always, by politics. Muslim Jew-hatred had traditionally lacked the virulent imagery found in Christian *Adversus Iudeous* rhetoric and European folklore, but Arab Christians imported those stereotypes into the Middle East. Customary religious vilifications became widespread after 1840, as Arabs identified Jews with modernism, commercialism, and imperialism; contemporary European anti-Semitism flourished as Zionism took root and the state of Israel materialized. Similarly, in the face of radical Islamism and Muslim hostility to Israel, many Christians and Jews wove long-standing disparagement of Islam as theologically deficient and Muslims as sociologically backward into Islamophobia, which vilified Muslims as mindlessly enslaved to a religion inherently committed to subduing or exterminating outsiders.

Assaults on religious minorities persisted everywhere, with the Holocaust standing as a particularly abhorrent example. Although Nazi anti-Semitism was arguably more racialist and nationalist than religious, it did condone violence against Jews as furthering God's war on evil, and it elicited support from Christian churches. Meanwhile, Egyptian Sunnis attacked Coptic Christians, and Iranian Shiites persecuted Baha'is. The struggle over Israel/Palestine—in which both Jews and Muslims held minority status depending on who drew the borders and when—was arguably a political disagreement, but religious identifications exacerbated the resentments. One of the most poignant consequences of these fights was the near-segregation of Jews and Muslims in the Middle East—the Abrahamic religions' birthplace—along with Christians' virtual disappearance from it.

Yet Jews, Christians, and Muslims still strove to improve their relationships, despite—or, perhaps, because of—their seemingly unrelenting enmities. The Holocaust's enormity triggered a crisis of conscience among churches contemplating Christianity's complicity in genocide. The most fateful reaction was the Second Vatican Council's promulgation in 1965 of *Nostra Aetate* ("In Our

The Abrahamic Religions

Time"), which asserted that "God holds the Jews most dear" and decried all "displays of anti-Semitism." It further allowed that other religions, including Islam, reflect a ray of truth, urging mutual conversation and cooperation, although it also presumed that the Church had little, if anything, to learn from other faiths. Pope Benedict XVI's invocation of a Byzantine emperor who accused Muhammad of condoning violence to spread Islam prompted an open letter originally endorsed by 138 prominent Muslims: "A Common Word Between Us and You" (2007). Taking its title from Quran 3:64, which solicits the "People of the Book" to acknowledge that they all worship God, this reply invited a range of Christian church leaders, not just Catholics, "to come together with us," averring that the world's future depends on its two largest religious communities fostering peace and justice. The most prominent Jewish response to *Nostra Aetate* was "Dabru

9. Mustafa Ceric, Grand Mufti of Bosnia, meets Pope Benedict XVI at the Vatican's first-ever Catholic–Muslim Forum, held in November 2008. Ceric was a signer of "A Common Word Between Us and You," an open letter addressed to Pope Benedict XVI that advocated dialogue between Muslims and Christians to promote peace and justice.

Emet" ("Speak Truth"), a statement authored privately by four university scholars, signed by more than 200 rabbis and intellectuals, and published in two American newspapers. Acknowledging the recent "unprecedented shift in Jewish and Christian relations," it affirmed that Jews and Christians worship the same God, that they accept the Torah's moral principles, and, most controversially among Jews, that "Nazism was not a Christian phenomenon."

"A Common Word" and "Dabru Emet" engineered bilateral conversations. But by the early twenty-first century, a diffuse sense was emerging in many quarters that, given the complex connections between Judaism, Christianity, and Islam, trilateral discussions might accomplish more. Oxford and Cambridge universities signaled budding academic recognition that the trio should be studied collectively by creating chairs in the field of the Abrahamic religions (both positions, intriguingly, funded by Muslim donors). As salutary as such efforts might be, however, comparative scholarship and top-level debates about interfaith issues will likely have little consequence absent parallel contacts among ordinary adherents. How often they break bread with each other, as opposed to fortifying local boundaries, will determine whether they live by the Golden Rule—an ideal the three religions share—or not.

Epilogue

Historical circumstances have colored both how members of the Abrahamic religions have constructed their identities and how they have regarded one another. Ruminating on the perceived connections between the traditions that the concept of the Abrahamic religions implies, contemporary proponents of interfaith engagement have sometimes fastened on Abraham—the eager host of three strangers who suddenly materialize outside his tent (Gen. 18:1)—as a model of how his self-proclaimed descendants might treat each other more generously than they have in the past. We can explore this proposition by examining two of the ways in which Judaism, Christianity, and Islam have historically colored their adherents' sense of identity: as individuals who may have an intimate connection to God; and as communities that have defined themselves in terms of their collective heritages. Such an exercise suggests that Abraham might in fact be a problematic figure for bringing Jews, Christians, and Muslims together. Ironically, they may come closer to inhabiting common spiritual ground when they seek God directly, shrugging off their ingrained religious identities, than when they define themselves as Abraham's kith and kin.

Adherents of the Abrahamic religions ordinarily pursue God through mediated means such as worship, prayer, or scripture reading, but their literatures also report instances of unitive

10. Abraham entertains the angels in Rembrandt's interpretation of the story in Genesis 18. The image of Abraham as generous host has been used to promote interfaith engagement among the three Abrahamic religions.

mysticism—the practice in which a believer enters into a transcendent union with the divine. Individuals have recounted such experiences in terms of communicating with, cleaving to, or dissolving into God while apprehending unfathomable wisdom or sublime love. Unitive mysticism can take distinctive forms in each religion, among them Kabbalistic practice in Judaism, individual visionary quests in Western Christianity, contemplative prayer in Eastern Orthodoxy, and Sufi disciplines in Islam. Yet, at the same time, the yearning for mystical union can blur doctrinal, legal, and sectarian boundaries, a condition that the Sufi Jalal ad-Din Rumi—whose death is said to have been lamented by Jews and Christians along with Muslims—celebrated:

> I am neither Christian, nor Jew, nor Gabr [Magian], nor Moslem....
> My place is the Placeless, my trace is the Traceless;
> 'Tis neither body nor soul, for I belong to the soul of the Beloved.

Jews, Christians, and Muslims utter some of their most similar religious sentiments when they speak of closing with God. They give voice to these unions in ways that seem to echo a shared religious desire.

But mystical experience is, by its nature, extremely personal. Adherents of the Abrahamic religions are less forthcoming about their commonalities when they identify their respective communities as Abraham's children. They revere Abraham and agree that he was remarkable for his absolute fidelity and obedience to God, as well as for having pronounced that God is One. Nevertheless, they also wrangle over how to construe and venerate him. Dissociating Abraham's insight about the One God of all humanity from his abhorrence of those who worship other gods or idols has proven hard in practice for *Am Yisrael*, the Body of Christ, and the *umma*. Each has displayed a tendency to deem itself Abraham's successor to the exclusion of everyone else. Jews regard him as a patriarch in a profoundly genetic sense, through whom God elects Israel. Christians consider themselves to be his rightful offspring, though they construe the genealogy spiritually. Muslims affirm an even stronger claim, asserting Islam's historical precedence and theological superiority to Judaism and Christianity. The Torah and Gospel were revealed only after Abraham, the Quran maintains; furthermore, he "was neither a Jew nor a Christian, but a hanif and a Muslim" (Qur. 3:67). Islam, by this reckoning, is not an Abrahamic religion but the religion of Abraham—its oldest, truest manifestation—and the *umma* are the people "worthiest" of him (Qur. 3:68). Confounding truth with error, the "People of the Book" see only through a dark glass.

Conceiving of Judaism, Christianity, and Islam as the Abrahamic religions calls attention to just how linked they are. Their overlapping histories and senses of identity refute notions that they belong to mutually alien civilizations. However, they are not perfectly congruent, nor do their likenesses necessarily predispose their adherents to put their differences aside. All of them celebrate their bonds with Father Abraham, but, in reconstructing family ties, remembrances of his lineage clash frequently. The stakes, after all, are high: sole possession of his legacy against the interests of competing heirs. Small wonder, then, that each party insists, "Dad always loved *me* best."

History has conditioned how members of the Abrahamic religions have interacted. They have shown capacities to mingle with—as well as maim—each other. Their braided futures will depend on how (or whether) they continue to contest their perceived birthrights.

References

Preface

"Abraham," "Abrahamic": *Oxford English Dictionary*, 3rd ed. (Oxford: Oxford University Press, 2009), https://oed.com/.

Chapter 1

"harmoniously": "The Treatise of St. Epiphanius...On Measures and Weights and Numbers and Other Things That Are in the Divine Scriptures," par. 6, http://www.tertullian.org/fathers/epiphanius_weights_03_text.htm#C9.

"every part": Flavius Josephus, *The Wars of the Jews*, bk. 6, chap. 5, par. 1, in *Josephus, Complete Works*, trans. William Whiston (1867; repr. Grand Rapids, MI: Kregel, 1981), 581.

Chapter 2

"'Hear not me'": Ronald E. Heine, *Montanist Oracles and Testimonia* (Macon, GA: Mercer University Press, 1989), 5.

"poison": Ignatius of Antioch, "The Epistle of Ignatius to the Trallians," 6.1–2, in *The Ante-Nicene Fathers: Translations of the Writings of the Fathers down to AD 325*, ed. Alexander Roberts and James Donaldson, 10 vols. (Edinburg: T. &. T. Clark, 1867–1872), 1:68.

"succession of bishops": Irenaeus, *Against Heresies*, III.3.2, in *Judaism, Christianity, and Islam: The Classical Texts and Their Interpretation*, ed. F. E. Peters, 3 vols. (Princeton, NJ: Princeton University Press, 1990), 1:323.

"most ancient church": Irenaeus, *Against Heresies*, III.3.2, in *Judaism, Christianity, and Islam: The Classical Texts and Their Interpretation*, ed. F. E. Peters, 3 vols. (Princeton, NJ: Princeton University Press, 1990), 1:323.

Chapter 3

"'By this conquer'": Eusebius, *Life of Constantine*, trans. Averil Cameron and Stuart G. Hall, Clarendon Ancient History Series (Oxford: Clarendon Press, 1999), 80 [1.28].

"consubstantial": Mark Edwards, "The First Council of Nicaea," in *The Cambridge History of Christianity*, 9 vols. (Cambridge: Cambridge University Press, 2006–2009), 1:561.

"before all ages": J. Skira, "Nicene–Constantinopolitan Creed: Comparison of Additions & Deletions," http://individual.utoronto.ca/jskira/PDF/Nicene-Constantinopolitan-Creed.pdf.

in "two natures": "The Fourth Ecumenical Council: The Council of Chalcedon, 451, *The Definition of Faith*," in *Creeds & Confessions of Faith in the Christian Tradition*, ed. Jaroslav Pelikan and Valerie Hotchkiss, 3 vols. (New Haven, CT: Yale University Press, 2003), 1:181.

"Moses speaking Attic Greek": Numenius of Apamea (fl. latter second century CE), in *Greek and Latin Authors on Jews and Judaism*, ed. Menahem Stern, 3 vols. (Jerusalem: Israel Academy of Sciences and Humanities, 1974–1984), 2:209–210.

"three titles": "Jerusalem Talmud Berakhot 9:1 (12d-13a)," in *Texts and Traditions: A Source Reader for the Study of Second Temple and Rabbinic Judaism*, ed. Lawrence H. Schiffman (Brooklyn, NY: KTAV Publishing House, 1997), 417.

Chapter 4

"ethical prophetic monotheism": Guy G. Stroumsa, *The Making of the Abrahamic Religions in Antiquity* (New York: Oxford University Press, 2015), 189–198.

"Jews have their religion": 'Abd al-Malik Ibn Hishām, *The Life of Muhammad: A Translation of Ishāq's* Sīrat Rasūl Allāh, ed. A[lfred] Guillaume (London: Oxford University Press, 1955), 233; citing a civil covenant—the so-called Constitution of Medina—that Muhammad promulgated for all the residents.

"Israelite tales": F. E. Peters, *Islam: A Guide for Jews and Christians* (Princeton, NJ: Princeton University Press, 2003), 16.

wept "copiously": From Abu Bakr al-Khwarazmi, *Maqtal al-Hoseyn*, quoted in Kamran Scot Aghaie, *The Martyrs of Karbala: Shi'i Symbols and Rituals in Modern Iran* (Seattle: University of Washington Press, 2004), 11.

Chapter 5

"fanciful notions": Sabih Ahmad Kamali, trans., *Al-Ghazali's Tahafut Al-Falasifah [Incoherence of the Philosophers]* (Lahore, Pakistan: Pakistan Philosophical Congress, 1963), 2.

"no god but God": Imam Muslim, *Sahih*, 1.6.20, in *Judaism, Christianity, and Islam: The Classical Texts and Their Interpretation*, ed. F. E. Peters, 3 vols. (Princeton, NJ: Princeton University Press, 1990), 2:357.

"soldiers of Christ": Fulcher of Chartres, *A History of the Expedition to Jerusalem 1095–1127*, trans. Frances Rita Ryan (Knoxville: University of Tennessee Press, 1969), 67.

"blood of the slain": Fulcher of Chartres, *History of the Expedition to Jerusalem*, 122.

Chapter 6

"nets": Martin Luther, "[The Ninety-Five Theses or] Disputation for Clarifying the Power of Indulgences," in *Martin Luther's Ninety-Five Theses*, ed. Timothy J. Wengert (Minneapolis: Fortress Press, 2015), 22 (thesis 66).

"strange, awkward, and new": Conyers Middleton, *Some Farther Remarks…* (London: n.p., 1752), 435, quoted in Jonathan Sheehan, *The Enlightenment Bible: Translation, Scholarship, Culture* (Princeton, NJ: Princeton University Press, 2005), 27.

"freedom to make *public use*": Immanuel Kant, "An Answer to the Question: 'What Is Enlightenment?,'" in *Kant: Political Writings*, ed. Hans Reiss, trans. H. B. Nisbet, 2nd ed. (Cambridge: Cambridge University Press, 1991), 55, emphasis in original.

"renewer" [one who will renovate]: Ahmad Hasan, trans., *Sunan Abu Dawud*, 3 vols. (Lahore, Pakistan: Sh. Muhammad Ashraf, 1984), vol. 3, bk. 32, chap. 1587, no. 4278, 1194.

"fail to impress": "The Pittsburgh Platform (1885)," in *Response to Modernity: A History of the Reform Movement in Judaism*, ed. Michael Meyer (Detroit, MI: Wayne State University Press, 1995), 388.

"latter-day Muslim": Youssef M. Choueiri, *Islamic Fundamentalism: The Story of Islamist Movements*, 3rd ed. (London: Continuum, 2010), 37.

Chapter 7

"heathen": Clement XI, "The Papal Bull of 1715 [Ex illa die]," art. V, in *China in Transition: 1517–1911*, ed. Dun J. Li (New York: Van Nostrand Reinhold, 1969), 23.

"inalienable right": Syed Qutb Shaheed, *Milestones*, trans. S. Badrul Hasan (Karachi, Pakistan: International Islamic Publishers, 1981), 143.

"religion and morality": [George Washington], "Washington's Farewell Address 1796," http://avalon.law.yale.edu/18th_century/washing.asp.

"Jud[e]o-Christian concept": "Eisenhower Tells of Zhukov Ouster," *New York Times*, December 23, 1952, 16, col. 5.

American Muslim population: Pew Research Center, "Pew–Templeton Global Religious Futures Project," http://www.globalreligiousfutures .org/religions/muslims. Some surveys would double or even triple this figure.

"God holds the Jews most dear": *Declaration on the Relation of the Church to Non-Christian Religions—Nostra Aetate*, proclaimed by Pope Paul VI (Vatican City: 1965), sec. 4 [par. 4, 7].

ray of truth: *Declaration on the Relation of the Church to Non-Christian Religions—Nostra Aetate*, sec. 2 [par. 2].

"come together": *A Common Word Between Us and You* (Jordan: Royal Aal al-Bayt Institute for Islamic Thought, 2009), 6, 8.

"unprecedented shift": National Jewish Scholars Project, "Dabru Emet: A Jewish Statement on Christians and Christianity," https://www.bc.edu/content/dam/files/research_sites/cjl/texts/ cjrelations/resources/documents/jewish/dabru_emet.htm.

Epilogue

"I am neither Christian": From Reynold A. Nicholson, ed. *Selected Poems from the Dîvîni Shamsi Tabrîz* (London: Cambridge University Press, 1898), repr. in William H. McNeil and Marilyn Robinson Waldman, eds., *The Islamic World* (New York: Oxford University Press, 1973), 242.

Further reading

Scriptures

Berlin, Adele, and Marc Zvi Brettler, eds. *The Jewish Study Bible: Jewish Publication Society TANAKH Translation*. New York: Oxford University Press, 2004.

Charles, R. H., ed. *The Apocrypha and Pseudepigrapha of the Old Testament in English*. 2 vols. Oxford: Clarendon Press, 1913.

Fakhry, Majid, trans. *An Interpretation of the Qur'an: English Translation of the Meanings: A Bilingual Edition*. New York: New York University Press, 2002.

Metzger, Bruce M., and Roland E. Murphy, eds. *The New Oxford Annotated Bible: With the Apocryphal/Deuterocanonical Books*. New York: Oxford University Press, 1991.

The William Davidson Talmud. Sefaria. https://www.sefaria.org/texts/Talmud.

Judaism

Batnitsky, Leora. *How Judaism Became a Religion: An Introduction to Modern Jewish Thought*. Princeton, NJ: Princeton University Press, 2011.

Cohen, Shaye. *From the Maccabees to the Mishnah*. 3rd ed. Louisville, KY: Westminster John Knox Press, 2014.

Jaffee, Martin S. *Early Judaism: Religious Worlds of the First Judaic Millennium*. 2nd ed. Bethesda: University Press of Maryland, 2006.

Meyer, Michael. *Response to Modernity: A History of the Reform Movement in Judaism*. Detroit, MI: Wayne State University Press, 1988. Reprint, 1995.

Satlow, Michael L. *Creating Judaism: History, Tradition, Practice.* New York: Columbia University Press, 2006.

Schwartz, Seth. *The Ancient Jews from Alexander to Muhammad.* Cambridge: Cambridge University Press, 2014.

Stanislawski, Michael. *Zionism: A Very Short Introduction.* New York: Oxford University Press, 2017.

Christianity

Allison, Dale C. *Constructing Jesus: Memory, Imagination, and History.* Grand Rapids, MI: Baker Academic, 2010.

Brubaker, Leslie. *Inventing Byzantine Iconoclasm.* London: Bristol Classical Press, 2012.

Jenkins, Philip. *Jesus Wars: How Four Patriarchs, Three Queens, and Two Emperors Decided What Christians Would Believe for the Next 1,500 Years.* New York: HarperOne, 2010.

Jenkins, Philip. *The Lost History of Christianity: The Thousand-Year Golden Age of the Church in the Middle East, Africa, and Asia—and How It Died.* New York: HarperOne, 2008.

Lieu, Judith. *Neither Jew nor Greek: Constructing Early Christianity.* London: T. & T. Clark, 2002.

MacCulloch, Diarmaid. *Christianity: The First Three Thousand Years.* New York: Viking Penguin, 2009.

Wandel, Lee Palmer. *The Reformation: Towards a New History.* New York: Cambridge University Press, 2011.

Islam

Asfaruddin, Asma. *The First Muslims: History and Memory.* Oxford: Oneworld Publications, 2008.

Berkey, Jonathan. *The Formation of Islam: Religion and Society in the Near East, 600–1800.* Cambridge: Cambridge University Press, 2011.

Choueiri, Youssef M. *Islamic Fundamentalism: The Story of Islamist Movements.* 3rd ed. London: Continuum, 2010.

Esposito, John L., and Natana J. Delong-Bas. *Shariah: What Everyone Needs to Know.* New York: Oxford University Press, 2018.

Haider, Najam. *Shiʿi Islam: An Introduction.* New York: Cambridge University Press, 2014.

Mattson, Ingrid. *The Story of the Qur'an: Its History and Place in Muslim Life.* 2nd ed. Chichester, UK: Wiley–Blackwell, 2013.

Silverstein, Adam J. *Islamic History: A Very Short Introduction.* Oxford: Oxford University Press, 2010.

Abrahamic religions

Bakhos, Carol. *The Family of Abraham: Jewish, Christian, and Muslim Interpretations.* Cambridge, MA: Harvard University Press, 2014.

Grabar, Oleg, and Benjamin Z. Kedar. *Where Heaven and Earth Meet: Jerusalem's Sacred Esplanade.* Jerusalem: Yad Ben Zvi Press, 2009.

Hughes, Aaron. *Abrahamic Religions: On the Uses and Abuses of History.* New York: Oxford University Press, 2012.

Levenson, John D. *Inheriting Abraham: The Legacy of the Patriarch in Judaism, Christianity & Islam.* Princeton, NJ: Princeton University Press, 2012.

Menocal, María Rosa. *Ornament of the World: How Muslims, Jews, and Christians Created a Culture of Tolerance in Medieval Spain.* Boston: Little, Brown, 2002.

Peters, F. E. *Judaism, Christianity, and Islam: The Classical Texts and Their Interpretation.* 3 vols. Princeton, NJ: Princeton University Press, 1990.

Peters, F. E. *The Monotheists: Jews, Christians, and Muslims in Conflict and Competition. Vol. 1: The Peoples of God.* Princeton, NJ: Princeton University Press, 2003.

Silverstein, Adam J., and Guy G. Stroumsa, eds. *The Oxford Handbook of the Abrahamic Religions.* Oxford: Oxford University Press, 2015.

Stroumsa, Guy G. *The Making of the Abrahamic Religions in Antiquity.* New York: Oxford University Press, 2015.

Comparative and other studies

Cohen, Charles L., Paul F. Knitter, and Ulrich Rosenhagen, eds. *The Future of Interreligious Dialogue: A Multireligious Conversation on Nostra Aetate.* Maryknoll, NY: Orbis Books, 2017.

Hillenbrand, Carole. *The Crusades: Islamic Perspectives.* Edinburgh: Edinburgh University Press, 1999.

Meddeb, Abdelwahab, and Benjamin Stora, eds. *A History of Jewish–Muslim Relations: From the Origins to the Present Day*. Translated by Jane Marie Todd and Michael B. Smith. Princeton, NJ: Princeton University Press, 2013.

Nirenberg, David. *Anti-Judaism: The Western Tradition*. New York: W. W. Norton, 2013.

Pew Research Center. "The Future of World Religions." Washington, DC: Pew Research Center, 2016. http://www.globalreligiousfutures.org/.

Pew Research Center. "The Global Religious Landscape: A Report on the Size and Distribution of the World's Major Religious Groups as of 2010." Washington, DC: Pew Forum on Religion & Public Life, 2012.

Polk, William R. *Crusade and Jihad: The Thousand-Year War between the Muslim World and the Global North*. New Haven, CT: Yale University Press, 2018.

Prothero, Steven. *God Is Not One: The Eight Rival Religions That Run the World*. New York: HarperOne, 2010.

Sorkin, David. *The Religious Enlightenment: Protestants, Jews, and Catholics from London to Vienna*. Princeton, NJ: Princeton University Press, 2008.

Index

For the benefit of digital users, indexed terms that span two pages (e.g., 52–53) may, on occasion, appear on only one of those pages.

The Abrahamic Religions